Dog Days of Summer

Racine, Wisconsin 2002

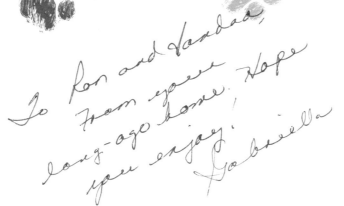

To Ron and Vandaa,
From your
long-ago home. Hope
you enjoy!
Gabriella

Written by Gabriella Klein

Photography by Brad Jaeck and Carol Hansen

Shown on the front cover are the canines that received
top prizes in the Dog Days of Summer competition. Left
to right are: *The Labrador of Lilliput,* created by Melanie
Pope, third place; *Dog Bone*, created by Linden Schulz,
second place; *Trojan Dog*, created by Renee Staeck,
first place. More information about all three is found
elsewhere in the book.

ISBN 1-59152-004-5
Photographs and text ©2002 Downtown Racine Corporation
Design by Sweetgrass Books, a Division of Farcountry Press

Created, produced, and designed in the United States.
Printed in Canada.

 # Acknowledgements

Like the Dog Days of Summer itself, this book started with Chicago's 1999 cows. In late February my husband Don was paging through the Cows on Parade in Chicago book and asked, "Why can't the dogs have a book like this?"

Why not, indeed!

When I volunteered to organize and write this book, Kathy Hansen, Downtown Racine Corporation's executive director, thought the idea was a good one.

When I asked Brad Jaeck and Carol Hansen of Photographic Design if their schedules could accommodate doing the photography, they found the time.

Dick Johnston, publisher of *The Journal Times*, a major Dog Days of Summer sponsor, suggested the graphic design and printing services of a Lee Enterprises division, Farcountry Press.

The book, like the event itself, was off and running. This was a team effort, believe me.

My thanks for excellent involvement from many people, including the artists and their wonderful creativity; Gene Johnson, who started the entire Dog Days of Summer experience; Downtown Racine Corporation's Kathy Hansen, executive director, and Brian Anderson, chairman; Bruce Pepich of Wustum Museum of Fine Arts/Racine Art Museum; the creative graphic design and production staff at Farcountry Press; and especially Brad Jaeck and Carol Hansen for their photography, attention to detail and commitment to this project; Terry Leopold of Downtown Racine Corporation for her organizational talents and proofing skills; and my husband for his encouragement and proofreading expertise.

Because of them—and many others—this book has become a reality and we all hope an enjoyable review of a very special time in Downtown Racine.

—Gabriella Klein

Contents

The Dogs Are Here!

A message from Kathy Hansen

Executive Director,
Downtown Racine Corporation

6

A year-long project unfolded in May, when the dogs hit the streets of Downtown Racine, and Dog Days of Summer arrived in our community.

This public art event took plenty of cooperation, drive, creativity and passion to bring to fruition. Every single person who touched this project played a key role in making it happen. And every single ounce of effort was well worth it, given the wonderful final results shown on 10 blocks of Main and Sixth streets in Downtown Racine and in this book.

Special thanks to Gene Johnson, who was the driving force behind the idea of Dog Days of Summer, and the person who did all the initial thinking and research to make sure we'd have dogs for our summer escapade.

Hearty kudos to our artists, who have been incredible, not only with their creativity—which you see on exhibit and in this book—but with their enthusiasm for making Dog Days a reality.

Bruce Pepich of Wustum Museum of Fine Arts/Racine Art Museum saw the merits of this public art event and he and his staff helped in many ways to bring Dog Days of Summer to the streets.

Dick Johnston and *The Journal Times* were on board from the beginning and also did much to help develop Dog Days of Summer.

Our sponsors came forth in droves, not only to sponsor dogs but also to help with things like sealcoating them for protection from the elements, making extensions for some of the dogs, and generally getting into the spirit of this Downtown event. Dog Days of Summer would not have happened without them.

Scores of DRC volunteers helped plan and carry out activities needed to support Dog Days of Summer—such as planning for and contributing to both the May 4 launch and the October 13 artists' party and auction; checking in finished dogs on April 9 and 16; transporting dogs between the DRC office and the "kennel" in the Johnson Building; and getting mailings prepared and sent out.

Seeger Map gave us great city maps so we could decide locations for our canines. Nordik of America made the wonderful dog-bone tags adjacent to the dogs, giving the names of the artist, the sponsor and the dog itself. People from Seater Construction helped in so many ways, including hauling dogs from place to place and making sure they were where they needed to be.

When the need for pull carts for 50 of our dogs became apparent, Grainger Industrial Supply came through with the carts at no charge, and community volunteer Mike Miklasevich and his associates assembled and painted the carts and then attached the canines.

I would like to thank Gabriella Klein who singlehandedly took on the responsibility of this book. Gabriella graciously volunteered her vision, writing talent, leadership and organizational skills to this project. She became part of the Downtown Racine Corporation family. We are very fortunate to have her.

And finally, many thanks to the Downtown Racine Corporation staff and board of directors, all who have been intimately involved in making Dog Days of Summer happen, and who I'm sure at times wondered if we'd ever get this wonderful project on the streets of Downtown Racine.

Downtown Racine definitely has gone to the dogs in the summer of 2002. Thanks to the hundreds of people who made this fun event a reality.

The Dog: Unleashed

A message from
Bruce W. Pepich

*Executive Director and
Curator of Collections,
Charles A. Wustum
Museum of Fine Arts*

Dogs can be found in artworks throughout the history of art from Egyptian tomb paintings to the present. Viewers can trace the development of the role of dogs in society by the way they are presented, and how this changes over time.

Prior to the 19th century, dogs were often used for symbolism, representing a range of attributes and frailties from fidelity and bravery to rudeness and unruly behavior. As dogs became an accouterment of the good life, they began to appear in sporting art in roles often reserved for prize horses.

As the presence of horses in modern life waned with the advance of the automobile and as people moved from farms to cities, dogs became more commonplace as pets in the households of the growing middle class. As dogs became more visible in modern life, they also began to appear more frequently in artworks. From inclusion in family oil portraits by Pierre-Auguste Renoir to contemporary photographs by William Wegman, dogs have moved from the edge of the work to center stage in the matter of a few decades. This is a direct reflection of the important roles they have in modern life.

The selection of dogs as the subject for Racine's first major public art project, The Dog Days of Summer, is further indication of the importance these animals have in our psyches. Our attraction to dogs is based on the many qualities we associate with them including playfulness, affection, dedication and a host of physical attributes that are both aesthetically pleasing and amusing.

Each of the artists in this exhibition has managed to transfer 149 identical sculptural forms into personal statements. Some participants present amusing literary and visual puns. Others have focused on the form of the animal, altering the original dog to fashion a creature with completely new, and sometimes surreal, associations. Some artists used the large flanks of these dogs as canvases on which to make paintings of the landscape or abstract compositions.

As wide-ranging as the many approaches to these Labradors may be, what unifies this exhibition is the consistent high quality found in all the works. The ideas expressed are witty. An overriding sense of care and craftsmanship predominates. That the bulk of artists selected are residents of the immediate area is a testament to our strong and active local visual arts community.

We thank the exhibiting artists, of a variety of ages and backgrounds, who have wholeheartedly thrown themselves into the challenge of this project. By unleashing their creativity, they have provided a new and positive meaning to the term "going to the dogs."

9

How Dog Days of Summer Started in Racine

Dog Days of Summer 2002 began during a conversation between husband and wife.

"Sam kept talking about getting more people Downtown," said Gene Johnson, the driving force behind getting Dog Days of Summer started. Mrs. Johnson is a longtime patron of the arts who also happens to love Downtown Racine and dogs (including the two Johnson dogs—Labrador Imie and Norwich terrier Titan).

"I thought about the Chicago cows," Mrs. Johnson said, and then I said, 'Why not dogs?'" She thought dogs would get people involved, they would be a draw for Downtown, and they could be a lot of fun.

A Chicago cow from the 1999 public art event there has been part of the Downtown Racine landscape since late fall of 1999, when Mrs. Johnson bought the cow—titled *And the Cow Jumped into the Moon*—at the Chicago cow auction and had it placed in front of Sam and Gene's Grotto at 336 Main Street.

This huge banner adorned the windows of the Downtown Racine Corporation office at 413 Main Street during the winter and spring.

Mrs. Johnson discussed the idea with Kathy Hansen, executive director of Downtown Racine Corporation. Hansen immediately took hold and the idea spread. Official sponsors for Dog Days of Summer are Downtown Racine Corporation, Racine Art Museum/Wustum Museum of Fine Arts and *The Journal Times*.

When Hansen approached Bruce Pepich, director of Racine Art Museum/Wustum Museum of

Gene Johnson and family canines Imie, left, and Titan enjoy an April walk on Downtown Racine's Main Street.

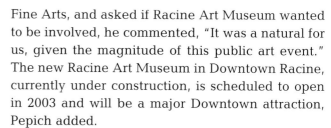

Downtown Chicago's Wisconsin Travel Information Center was graced with the presence of Little Dog Laughed, *who helped advertise Downtown Racine's Dog Days of Summer. The sculpture, commissioned by Gene Johnson, was created by Bill Reid of Racine.*

Fine Arts, and asked if Racine Art Museum wanted to be involved, he commented, "It was a natural for us, given the magnitude of this public art event." The new Racine Art Museum in Downtown Racine, currently under construction, is scheduled to open in 2003 and will be a major Downtown attraction, Pepich added.

"Gene was the driving force behind Dog Days of Summer," Hansen said. "She did a ton of work getting this going. And she's stayed with us through the entire year-long process of turning the idea into a reality."

In fact, Mrs. Johnson is one of the members of the steering committee overseeing the entire Dog Days experience. Others are Hansen; Pepich; Lisa Englander and Annie Horvath, both from Wustum; and Richard Johnston, publisher of *The Journal Times.*

Where Will We Find the Dogs?

It's wonderful to have an idea about a public art exhibition using dogs. But where does one find the dogs to be used?

"This was a hard part," according to Mrs. Johnson. "I had no idea. Then I happened to read an article in the *Chicago Tribune* about the company called Cowpainters, which develops fiberglass sculptures. I contacted them to see if they could help us."

Cowpainters bills itself as an upbeat art studio specializing in the creation and custom design of whimsical fiberglass animals. It provides animals and consultations for public art events and other activities. It was ready to help.

Mrs. Johnson and Cowpainters went to work. "They had several dogs we could choose from. The

Sixth Street west from the intersection of Main and Sixth is one of two Downtown Racine streets to be graced with public-art canines.

mold for the seated lifesize Labrador existed. We also wanted a standing Lab for variety's sake," according to Mrs. Johnson. Several molds later, an approved mold was made.

The standing lab is 30 inches high, 36 inches long and 9 inches wide. Its seated companion measures 25 inches high, 28 inches long and 12 inches wide. The average weight is 25 pounds; weights vary because each dog has been hand-made.

Cowpainters helped Mrs. Johnson and the Dog Days committee develop the criteria for painting and otherwise embellishing and protecting the dogs so they would withstand more than five months on exhibit.

Initially, the steering committee thought about an event of 50 dogs. "As word spread about what we were doing," Hansen said, "it was obvious 50 dogs were definitely not enough. Interest in the whole project grew very quickly." The decision was made to commit for 150 dogs, 149 that would be developed for the public event and one that would be sold—naked—at the Dog Days of Summer debut event in May 2002.

Other Planning

The DRC staff and dozens of volunteers had their planning work cut out for them, according to Hansen. "Many facets are involved in a project of this scope," she said. "We needed to propose the event to the City of Racine and secure its approval.

13

Downtown Racine's Main Street is ready for an exciting 2002 summer, complete with banners installed in the entire Downtown area in early May.

We had to develop a marketing plan and then address other activities."

These included developing rules for the artists, including the legal release forms; finding sponsors; getting Downtown retailers involved; working with *The Journal Times* to develop the Web site; finding a place to store the dogs prior to their exhibition; planning both the initial May 4 debut and the October 13 artists' party and auction.

Much of the planning needed to be done immediately, Hansen said, while some progressed as the dogs were being created. Everything had to be in place by the time the dogs made their first public appearance May 4.

The first shipment of 50 white, fiberglass and resin dogs arrived in Racine on Tuesday, November 6, 2001. The remaining 100 arrived several days later.

Dog Days of Summer was truly on its way.

Cows/Dogs, Chicago/Racine

Downtown Racine's dogs have ties to Chicago's cows of 1999. Chicago's cow parade started the thought process for Dog Days of Summer. And an age-old nursery rhyme further ties it all together.

Hey Diddle Diddle
The cat and the fiddle,
The cow jumped over the moon.
The little dog laughed to see such sport,
And the dish ran away with the spoon.

This nursery rhyme inspired the bovine, *And the Cow Jumped into the Moon*, created for Chicago's Adler Planetarium and ultimately purchased at auction by Gene Johnson. The cow now resides on the sidewalk in front of 336 Main Street, Racine.

Ronit Mitchell designed and created *And the Cow Jumped into the Moon*. When she and husband Scott Bullock, owners of Chicago's Penumbra Studios, heard about the plans for Racine's Dog Days of Summer, they knew they wanted to build on Mitchell's 1999 creation. They submitted

Laughing Dog
Artists: Ronit Mitchell
and Scott Bullock
Sponsor: Johnson Outdoors

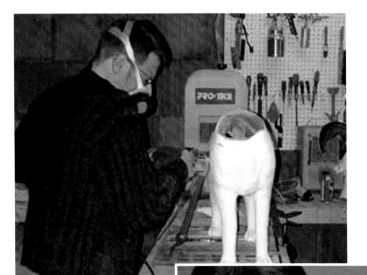

their design idea, it was approved, and *Laughing Dog* was born.

"This was a natural for us," explained Mitchell when she and Bullock delivered *Laughing Dog* to Racine. "And we had such fun with it. Nursery rhymes are wonderful—so whimsical, so much imagination."

Constructing *Laughing Dog* and the accompanying fleeing dish and spoon was no quick or simple process.

"The biggest challenge was pulling him apart and putting him back together again," Bullock explained, "so the now-standing dog would be as close to anatomically correct as possible and would exist indefinitely in his new configuration." This process alone took more than two weeks.

Creativity and durability continued to the fleeing plate and spoon.

"With the plate and spoon," Mitchell said, "we used a real plate and spoon. We had to make sure they were strong elements and would withstand being on display."

Laughing Dog's personality was easier to achieve. "He was such fun to have in the studio," according to Mitchell. "If I was having a stressed or bad day, all I had to do was look at him and I couldn't help but smile."

Mitchell calls her personal fine artwork "seeking the

Scott Bullock spent more than two weeks restructuring the Labrador from its four-legged stance to its final two-leg configuration, making sure the final result is as anatomically correct as possible.

muse," with the attempt to "constantly recognize, celebrate and encourage the play of the human spirit," she said. "In jester hat and playful stance, *Laughing Dog* captures this essence," Mitchell continued, adding that "Racine's Dog Days of Summer are also a great example of recognizing this spirit."

The young artists founded Penumbra Studios more than three years ago, right before the cow opportunity presented itself. They had met while working at a Chicago art store. They both then attended Chicago's American Academy of Art. "We were in school together and we had worked together. All this seemed like the natural flow of our lives," Mitchell explained.

Ronit Mitchell enjoys creating the playful personality of Laughing Dog.

When discussing Penumbra Studios, Mitchell explained, "We create great spaces while enriching the human spirit. We specialize in murals, trompe l'oeils and high-end finishes." Among their commissions have been those for Adler Planetarium, Marshall Field's and East Bank Club.

As fine artists, included in Mitchell's and Bullock's many exhibitions have been those at Sotheby's The Three Arts Club, University Club of Chicago and Byron Roche Gallery.

About Racine

Mitchell and Bullock rave about Racine, which they've visited five or six times. "I love the total feel when I come here," Mitchell said. The fact that *And the Cow Jumped into the Moon* now lives here only adds to that feel, according to Bullock.

After Chicago's cow parade ended in the fall of 1999, the cows were sold at auction. Mitchell had no idea who had purchased her creation. It was on a trip to Racine in November of 2001 that she found out.

"We were doing a project here for a client," Bullock explained. "We were heading out for dinner and were driving down Main Street. I looked ahead and said, 'That looks like a cow.'"

"As we got closer," Mitchell continued, "we saw it was my cow. We were ecstatic! Stunned!"

Joining the cow on Main Street for Dog Days of Summer is *Laughing Dog* and the accompanying runaway dish and spoon.

Ronit Mitchell unfolds Laughing Dog's *jester cap while husband Scott Bullock steadies the standing dog.*

18

The Artistic Selection Process

When a call for design proposals for Dog Days of Summer went out in 2001, staff from Downtown Racine Corporation, Wustum Museum of Fine Arts/Racine Art Museum and *The Journal Times*, the event's sponsoring organizations, didn't really know what to expect.

"We weren't sure what we'd receive," said Bruce Pepich, executive director of Wustum Museum of Fine Arts and the Racine Art Museum now under construction in Downtown Racine.

"The response was overwhelming," he said. "We received more than 400 proposals for the 149 dogs we had available for decoration.

"I always said Racine has a strong art community. But this was incredible."

How do you whittle 400 down to 149? "It was not an easy process for our review panel," according to Pepich. "The ideas were so diverse; we had a very broad range of styles and approaches—from paint to collage and sculpture, even adding elements to the existing dogs."

A panel of six experts split into two teams. They reviewed the designs to make sure they met the basic criteria—appropriate for public display for people of all ages, especially geared toward children and families; no corporate logos or advertising; no religious, political or controversial messages.

"Then the panel members applied additional critical criteria," Pepich explained. "Will the dog look good aesthetically? Do they think the artist can execute the concept? Will the dog withstand more than five months on public display, or are there maintenance issues to be addressed?"

Several artists submitted multiple designs, according to Pepich. In some instances, more than one concept was approved for creation. In others, the design the artist was sure would be approved was not, but another design was.

"When I saw the dogs as they were being delivered in April, I was blown away," Pepich said. "I knew our panelists had made excellent selections but when I saw the work of the artists I was amazed.

"This whole thing is incredible!"

Doing the Dog

ow does an artist create an entry for Dog Days of Summer?

Think up a design. Put it on paper. Get the dog from Downtown Racine Corporation. Paint the dog.

And that's it, right? Wrong!

The process for creating a dog that's part of the Dog Days of Summer public art event was a long and sometimes arduous one. Many requirements had to be met before an artist could actually even begin to work on the dog itself.

A call for design ideas went out in the fall of 2001. Those who wanted to submit ideas received a multi-page packet of materials to help guide them through the idea-submission process.

The artist first needed to complete a proposal form, giving personal information and outlining the idea for the dog. On an accompanying form was an actual outline of the dog—either seated or standing. The artist was required to sketch the design idea onto that form and submit it along with the proposal form.

Initial Ideas

Artists were encouraged to develop designs that were "creative, unique, playful." Where did they get their ideas? From everywhere.

Meg Daniels, who created *Frank Lab Wright*, happens to be a Frank Lloyd Wright fan. Her design came from Wright's windows in the Avery Coonley playhouse. "I chose these windows for inspiration because they were some of Wright's favorites, and for their playfulness," Daniels said, noting that "with these windows Wright incorporated more circular forms and a bolder primary palate."

Pat King, artist for *Chili Dawg*, said, "For the last several years I have been finding myself leaning toward subjects from the natural world, particularly sea life, for sources of inspiration."

Celestial Dog's creator, Stephen Samerjan, wrote, "A summer night's points of light present armatures upon which cultures have built narrative and visual structures crafted of the imagination, story forms which, when recounted generation to generation, connect us across time and culture with one another."

"My father taught me a lot about astronomy and the idea of a 'sun dog' always appealed to me as I was growing up," explained Julie Lalor, creator of *Sun Dog*.

Ellen Gutknecht, who developed *Tiedo*, did so as

Left: *Sandy Schmitz uses a human wig to fashion a hairstyle for* Ain't Nothin' but a Hound Dog.

Below: *Cecilia Schmidt applies more home-grown and preserved flowers and continues the design on* Bou-K-9.

Sally Orth and Terry Leopold work on Flower Pup. *Orth's kitchen table became the creative center for developing this canine.*

event, people would be touching the dogs, so the canines needed to be able to withstand contact. In other words, durability and public safety had to play roles in the design's development.

Many of the dogs would be displayed outdoors, right on the street. So they needed to be able to withstand all kinds of weather—from rain to hot sun to high humidity—and everything else summer brings to Downtown Racine.

Finally, if a dog should be damaged in any way, the artist needed to be available to do repair work. If he or she would not be available, then another artist would be asked for help.

an art enrichment lesson for her elementary art students. "Bringing the dog to school and discussing the paint, techniques, and brainstorming was a wonderful way to introduce them to public art."

When developing design ideas, the artists needed to keep in mind the fact that the audience for their dogs would be broad-based and of all ages, so the dogs had to be appropriate for public display. No advertising or corporate logos were allowed.

Because Dog Days of Summer is an interactive

Transforming the Dog

Artists were given preparation and painting hints as they began the transformation process. While the dogs were primed and ready for painting, it was recommended they be underpainted with a coat of acrylic titanium white paint diluted with a specific medium.

Artists went to work. Many spent several weeks

Left: Peg Ducommun's 13-year-old Lyndi exhibits patience and even resignation while Raider *is being created.*

Below: Many area firms provided support for dogs as they were being created for *Dog Days of Summer.* A-1 Auto Body donated the final clear coats to dozens of the dogs. Shown applying clear-coating, to protect the dogs from wear and weather, are A-1 employees Marty Schlegel and David Peterson.

transforming their dogs into works of public art. They ran into challenges, of course. Some found what they had envisioned in a two-dimensional drawing would not translate to the contours of the dog's three-dimensional body. Design adjustments had to be made.

Some design executions just did not work. Frank Deracin, when creating *Meowzer*, ran into problems. "I really thought this would be a great opportunity to play with 'camera obscura,'" he said. "The distortions and forshortening from superimposing a cat image upon a dog form were too strange, to say the least….So I sculpted a cat mask, cast it in fiberglass and coated it with tissue and gesso to give it that whimsical papier mache look."

Violet O'Dell's *Found Friends* caused her frustration. "I was just going nuts trying to figure out where to attach some of the other animals so they'd stay in place." She woke up one morning with the solution—attach

them to the feet, where they would be relatively safe.

As LeeAnn Morelli was finishing up her *Dog and Suds*, she realized the latex foam she was using for the suds would disintegrate when the final coating was put on the dog. So she had to remove the foam and then reapply it when the coating was finished and dry.

Because the dogs would be outdoors and on exhibit for more than five months before being sold at auction October 13, they needed to be varnished when finished, and then clear-coated, preferably with an auto body clear coat. Racine's auto body shops were busy in early April as the dogs were being completed.

Creating a dog for Dog Days of Summer was a long, time-consuming process—and the results show the value of what the artists experienced as they worked to share their talents with the public.

Sponsors a Key to Success

For Dog Days of Summer to be successful as a fund-raiser for both Downtown Racine Corporation and Racine Art Museum, sponsorship was needed to pay for the $250 cost of each dog, in addition to $100 to go to the artist for supplies to create the finished dog.

A call for sponsors went out in the fall of 2001. By spring of 2002, all dogs had sponsors, with several organizations sponsoring more than one canine.

Sponsors came from the expected resources—area businesses and organizations. But sponsorship did not stop there.

In some instances, sponsors encouraged artists to submit their ideas, assuring them sponsorship if their ideas were selected. Grandparents sponsored grandchildren. Parents sponsored children. Families sponsored other family members.

Some sponsors selected the dogs they wanted to support by going through the approved design proposals. Others indicated they wanted to sponsor a dog but were not particular about which one.

A total of 132 different sponsors have supported pooches in Dog Days of Summer. A complete index of canine sponsors is found on page 144.

Follow the Yellow Brick Road

When Jayne Miner of Racine designed *The Wizard of Dogz*, little did she know her creation for Dog Days of Summer would lead to fun and creativity of a different sort in the student services department at Gateway Technical College's Racine campus.

"We wanted to sponsor a dog and we wanted to have some fun," explained Sandie Bachmann. She and the other staff people in the department—Jo Bailey, Debby Burke, Bonnie Friday, Liz Nielsen, Pat Patriarca and Carmen Rigau—got to work.

Artist Jayne Miner, seated right, meets with members of Gateway's student services staff, who generated the sponsorship of The Wizard of Dogz. *Seated left is Pat Patriarca; standing from left are Liz Nielsen, Bonnie Friday, Jo Bailey, Debby Burke and Sandie Bachmann.*

"A few of us reviewed the approved designs and selected *The Wizard of Dogz,*" Bachmann explained. "Then came the challenge—how to pay the $350 sponsorship fee."

That's when the creativity really took off. First staff members formed the Over the Rainbow Kennel Club. Then they put together a program to sell shares in Ruby, the name they had given the dog.

People—more than 30 of them, both at Gateway's Racine campus and elsewhere—responded and became stockholders.

Stockholder recognition depended on the level of

participation. All recognition items were devised by the seven women. For one share, $3, the person received a certificate. Two shares, $5, brought a certificate and a specially designed pin. Three shares, $7, yielded the certificate, the pin, and a foam-core-mounted illustration of Ruby in the stockholder's office for a day. Ten dollars brought the stockholder the certificate, the pin, Ruby's likeness in the office for a day, and a pair of ruby slippers.

Major stockholders, at $30, received all the items, plus a framed picture of *Ruby, The Wizard of Dogz.*

All stockholders also became members of the Over the Rainbow Kennel Club.

But the fun didn't stop there. The seven also made sure special events were part of the stockholder benefits. There was a meet-the-artist reception in March; an article in the *Gateway Gazette*, the campus newspaper, in April; a group picture with the dog in its Downtown setting in May; and a June evening Downtown stroll, with a stop for refreshments, to view all the dogs in Dog Days of Summer.

Was the group successful in raising its needed $350 to sponsor *The Wizard of Dogz*? "Yes, we were," Bachmann said. "We needed to raise more, of course, because we had to pay for our promotional expenses. And, we did just fine."

Above: *Debby Burke creates ruby red slippers, a gift item for those who buy a certain number of stocks in* The Wizard of Dogz. *Burke made 31 pairs of the famous slippers.*

Right: *Assorted promotional materials, including a doggie portrait, a stock certificate, an invitation and a promotional brochure, helped raise funds to support the sponsorship of* The Wizard of Dogz.

A Project in Process

Prairie Dog (In His Wright Mind)
Artists: City of Racine Main Gallery Young Artists Program—
Katie Gebhardt, Jarrod Johnson, Cory Tuinstra; artist-in-
residence Jane Hobbs-Cascio
Sponsor: Jensen Metal Products

All art is a work in process. And when it comes to going from a two-dimensional design to a three-dimensional finished product, the process becomes even more important.

This is one of the lessons three teen artists learned when creating *Prairie Dog (In His Wright Mind)* for Racine's Dog Days of Summer.

This dog, sponsored by Jensen Metal Products, was designed by Jane Hobbs-Cascio of Racine, an artist-in-residence for the City of Racine Main Gallery Young Artists Program. Main Gallery, founded here in 1995, employs young people ages 14 to 21 to work on city-wide art projects.

When the design was accepted as one of the final 149 for Dog Days of Summer, three of her Main Gallery artists took over to make the dog a reality. They are Katie Gebhardt, 15, a student at Washington Park High School; Jarrod Johnson, also 15, and Cory Tuinstra, 16, both students at Walden III.

Hobbs-Cascio's original design called for several Frank Lloyd Wright architectural works to cover the dog, including Racine's Wingspread and suburban Chicago's Hardy House, as well as a Wright stained glass window at the Arizona Biltmore Hotel in

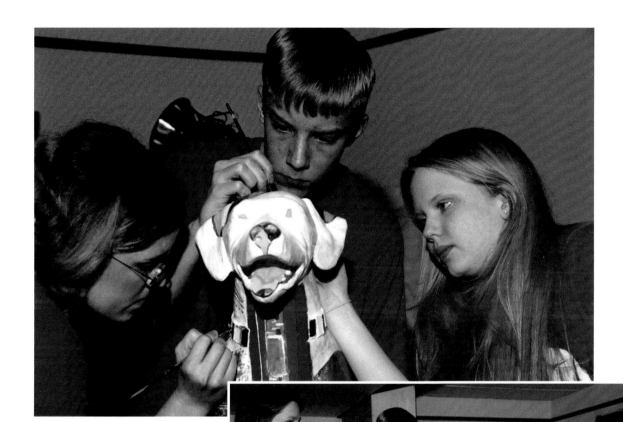

Above: *Katie Gebhardt, Jarrod Johnson and Cory Tuinstra work on tiny detail of* Prairie Dog.

Right: *Artist-in-residence Jane Hobbs-Cascio and her Main Gallery artists solve a problem in* Prairie Dog's *design.*

Backsides can be beautiful!

Phoenix, and of course elements from the SC Johnson building in Racine, including the Great Work Room and the Research Tower.

"Then the kids got started. And they found out things wouldn't necessarily work," Hobbs-Cascio said. "So they had to make major adjustments."

Wingspread and Hardy House simply would not conform to the contours of the dog. Instead, the trio incorporated Falling Water, Wright's masterpiece at Mill Run, Pennsylvania.

"I did not touch this dog," Hobbs-Cascio emphasized. "These three did the work. It's amazing how much the dog has changed from the original design. These kids have been open to experimentation. They noticed what needed to be done—and they did it."

Hobbs-Cascio points with pride to her three teen artists, who spent about six weeks working on the dog. "They're diligent, creative, and very committed to this project."

The trio admits its greatest challenge was crowding. "Three on a dog at once is difficult," according to Cory. They agree, however, that working together was tremendously helpful, especially when it came to solving design problems.

All three have worked together before. They were among the group of 14 who in the summer of 2001 painted a huge mural at Historic Century Market on Sixth Street in Downtown Racine. All three plan to stay in the Main Gallery program until they're 21 years old and no longer eligible.

All have a consuming interest in art and hope to pursue it as adults. Jarrod, in addition to working on the dog during spring break, also was painting a 20 x 7-foot scenic mural at a Kenosha nursing home. Cory has been painting murals at Walden III School in Racine. And Katie has done murals at McKinley Middle School in Racine.

It's obvious when watching these three teens work that they know how to solve creative challenges as part of the development process—and have fun at the same time.

The Dogs Come from School

The Dog Days of Summer, and its creative challenges, provided plenty of activity in several Racine public and private schools. Students competed in design contests. They learned how to create in two dimensions but implement in three. They learned how to manage their time so their dogs would be delivered by the April 16 deadline. And most of all, they and their art instructors had fun with the projects.

Here are brief looks at some of the school projects.

Carrying On History with Stephen Bull Dog

When you have a school named after a historic Racine figure, it only makes sense to have a dog carry on the same name.

That was the thinking when Stephen Bull Fine Arts School Principal Angela Apmann began developing the identity for *Stephen Bull Dog*, the school's entry for Dog Days of Summer.

These 11 fifth graders at Stephen Bull Fine Arts Elementary School worked for several weeks on painting and outfitting Stephen Bull Dog. From left are David Bloom, Nathan Matson, Alex Paul, Brianna Chu, Robert Williams, Kattie Browne, Lucy Haas, Randi Meinert, Kristy Steinpas, Jacob Olsen and Harrison Mattheis.

The school, a magnet school within Racine Unified School District, was founded in 1975. Its program emphasizes the fine arts—art, drama, dance and music—as an integral part of a child's education within the structure of a sound academic program.

Brianna Chu fits braces into Stephen Bull Dog's mouth. Ultimately the dog's braces have rubber bands in the school's colors: teal and purple.

Lisa Johnson, who has been the art instructor at Fine Arts School since 1979, and the 11 fifth graders in her art studio class then set to work creating the dog. They met for 45 minutes every Tuesday and Thursday afternoon and for several weeks their energies went to the dog.

How do you dress a dog? "This was not easy," Johnson said. "We bought clothing but then it needed to be adjusted for the dog." And that's where Pam Goerger, Fine Arts librarian since 1985, came into the picture. Goerger is a seamstress and she made the "alterations" for *Stephen Bull Dog's* attire.

Stephen Bull Dog

Artists: Lisa Johnson and Fine Arts Students
Sponsor: Stephen Bull Fine Arts Elementary School

The students had the most challenges when it came to painting and outfitting the dog. They reported about difficulty painting his teeth, which ultimately were fitted with braces and with brace rubber bands in the school colors—teal and purple. They shared the fact that the dog's eyes "looked funny" so they needed to be filed down. They agreed putting glasses on *Stephen Bull Dog* made him look older than a fifth grader. And his shoes needed to be cut to accommodate the shape of his paws.

The students had the most fun with Stephen's backpack. They brought a variety of backpacks to school for consideration. And they worked hard to gather the items for his backpack—notebook, pencils, markers, an apple.

"We wanted to make sure we had items in that backpack representing the fine arts and our curriculum," Johnson explained. "We have a script from the drama department, a book from the library, ballet shoes from the dance area, markers and crayons from the art department and a kazoo from the music room.

"After all," Johnson said, "one of the functions of art is to create community. We're certainly doing that with *Stephen Bull Dog*."

That sense of community reached throughout the entire school, which had 325 kindergarten through fifth grade students in 2001-2002.

"All our students and staff have been involved," according to Apmann. She explained she conducted school-wide student fund-raisers, with the goal of purchasing Stephen Bull Dog at the auction in October. "We have no idea how much we'll need, but we're working hard to raise enough money," Apmann said. "We want *Stephen Bull Dog* back here where he belongs."

St. Catherine's High School Art Students Go to—Three Dogs

About 50 students at St. Catherine's High School, Racine, got into the act when it came to participating in Dog Days of Summer.

Lisa Johnson, art instructor, and Pam Goerger, librarian, proudly pose with Stephen Bull Dog.

"My art students all generated designs, as did other SCHS students," according to Julie Lynam, art instructor and student activities director. "A judging panel then selected three and sent those in for competition. We were happy—all three were chosen."

"We were fortunate to have help from others outside the school also," said Celeste Henken, SCHS development director. She mentioned technical expertise and supplies from Jensen Metal Products, Metal World, Color Arts, Ruud Electric and Kortendick's Ace Hardware.

Implementing the creation of the designs became the goal. During a Tuesday early evening in March, the basement art area at SCHS seemed to be in total disarray to the visitor. Appearances were deceiving, however, as it became clear that each dog was being transformed into its final artwork. Students came and went, and put their touches on the three critters.

"Someone said 'What about food?' and that got things going," said SCHS senior John Kasprzak, the lead creative person developing *Doggie Bag*, sponsored by Quizno's Downtown. "The dog evolved from there." The canine was covered with foam, then edible items were carved from the foam and painted. John is attending Art Institute of Schaumburg, Illinois, in fall 2002, majoring in media arts and animation.

Sophomore Molly Pekar's design was in tribute to the dogs who helped following September 11. "I like dogs and I wanted to recognize these special dogs," she said of *All Dogs Go to Heaven*, sponsored by St. Catherine's Anonymous Alumni.

The most difficult part of creating the dog? "Trying to decide how I want the spots," she said. She also pointed out a subtle Mickey Mouse ear as one of the spots "because I like going to Disney World."

Molly Pekar works on making sure her dog has the right intensity of color on its nose.

All Dogs Go to Heaven
*Artist: Molly Pekar and
SCHS Art Students
Sponsored by St. Catherine's
Anonymous Alumni*

America, designed by freshman Amy Hantschel and the SCHS Key Club and sponsored by Project Management Associates, also was in reaction to September 11. Money generated by the Key Club and other SCHS clubs and departments during the 2001-2002 school year has been donated to the September 11 Scholarships for Surviving Children's Fund, Amy explained, adding that the dog *America* symbolizes hope and happiness for those children.

Amy, who hopes to make art her career, enjoys drawing and said

Doggie Bag
Artist: John Kasprzak and
SCHS Art Students
Sponsored by Quizno's Downtown

Above: *Applying foam and plenty of it is John Kasprzak's first step in developing Doggie Bag.*

Right: *SCHS art instructor Julie Lynam, second from left, reviews her students' work with, from left, Molly Pekar, John Kasprzak and Amy Hantschel.*

Amy Hantschel and her pooch seem to have formed a bond during the dog's development.

America
Artist: Amy Hantschel and SCHS Key Club
Sponsored by Project Management Associates

she was having no problems painting the dog. She did express relief, on behalf of all the SCHS artists, that the right color for the dogs' tongues was finally achieved, after several tries.

Meet a R.E.A.L. Dog

A class assignment turned into *A R.E.A.L. Dog* for two seniors at The R.E.A.L. (Racine Educational Alternative Learning Environment) School, a charter school within the Racine Unified School District. Opened as a full day school in September 2001 after a year as a part-time afternoon school, The R.E.A.L. School serves 127 sixth through 12th graders.

When the Dog Days of Summer project was announced, Phil Williams, head of the school's art program, saw a student opportunity: conduct a contest for the best dog design, then submit it for consideration for Dog Days of Summer. *A R.E.A.L. Dog* was one of the 149 designs selected.

Senior Ellen Kinzelman designed *A R.E.A.L. Dog*. She describes her dog artwork as "a flowing design with stark use of color." She incorporated the school's light blue and navy blue colors into the teardrop pattern covering the entire dog.

Joining her on the project was senior April Neau. This was not the first time—and probably not the last time—this pair has undertaken a collaborative project. During Racine's Make a Difference Day in October 2001, they did a mural of Noah's Ark on the wall of an area church. Classroom murals for The R.E.A.L. School also are in the plans for this artistic pair.

The duo agrees the biggest challenge in designing and painting the dog was transferring a two-dimensional idea into a three-dimensional format. They report they learned a lot while doing the project.

The dog's sponsor, A-1 Auto Body, played a major role in the project. The firm did the required base spray on the dog's body, then did the clear-coating

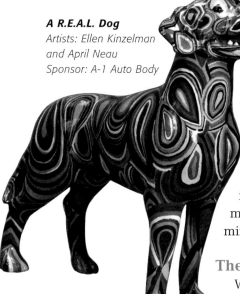

A R.E.A.L. Dog
*Artists: Ellen Kinzelman
and April Neau
Sponsor: A-1 Auto Body*

when the painting was finished. Both steps were part of the requirements in developing a dog for Dog Days of Summer.

Ellen is heading to art school in the fall of 2002. Though she loves art, April is looking at a career in the medical field, with a minor in Spanish.

The Two-in-One Dog

Walden III within the Racine Unified School District is both a middle and high school. So it's only appropriate that its dog represent both Walden III segments.

That was the thinking that went into the creation of *Underdog/Dog #98765*, according to Alex Mandli, art instructor.

Mandli explained the school ran a competiton for a design for a dog from Walden III. Following the competition, staff decided to have a dual dog—one from the middle school, the other from the high school.

"We had many good designs," Mandli explained. "We needed to pick designs we thought would go together on one dog."

Alex Tompsett is the artist for the Underdog portion of the dog. A sophomore at Walden III, he created the muscular structure because he wanted a way to incorporate the colors of the rainbow, which

*Ellen Kinzelman, standing, who created the design for
A R.E.A.L. Dog, and April Neau work on painting tricky areas on
the canine creation.*

also are the Walden III school colors. "The color was the start of my design. Then I found something that would use colors," Alex said. In his initial design submission, he had the muscular structure of a cat because he had not located one for a dog. The finished product, however, is a dog's structure.

Alex enjoys spending time outdoors and drawing with pencils. His favorite subject? "Mostly animals," he said.

Eighth grader Zachariah Fudge thought "a dog with gears and hydraulics would look interesting. I also think it gives a message against discarding something that works fine when something new arises."

Zach hopes to pursue art as a career. He's into ceramics—both creation and decoration—in a major way. In fact, during spring break this year, he was working not only on *Dog #98765* but also on finishing a chess set.

In working on the dog, the students worked both together and independently, with the dog traveling between their houses and school.

The biggest challenges in developing this dual dog? "Time was a real challenge for me," Zach said. "I had so many other things I was doing."

For Alex, the greatest challenge was "working with somebody else." He agrees the shared experience, however, has been a good one for him.

Zachariah Fudge and Alex Tompsett pose with their dual-identity dog.

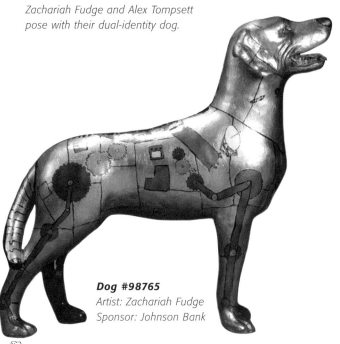

Dog #98765
Artist: Zachariah Fudge
Sponsor: Johnson Bank

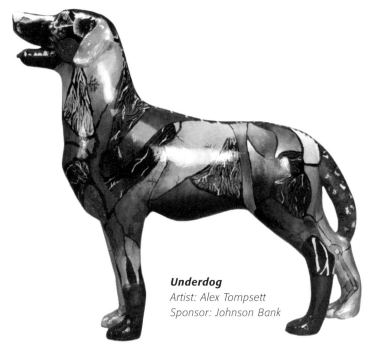

Underdog
Artist: Alex Tompsett
Sponsor: Johnson Bank

The Days of Departure

Dog and Suds *and its creator, LeeAnn Morelli, drive up to the dog delivery point at the Johnson Building.*

Fiberglass dogs in varying stages of creative development had been at home for several months in the residences and studios of their creators. But the days of this comfort were growing short and the day of departure—either April 9 or 16—was coming close.

On those two April days, the basement of the new Johnson Building in Downtown Racine became the departure point for the decorated canines and their creators. A section of the basement of that new building was turned into a kennel, as the canines were stored there until their first public showing May 4, and their subsequent display on Main and Sixth streets in Downtown Racine starting May 7.

When artists dropped off their dogs on warm, sunny April 16, they had to drive through construction barricades and rerouted streets to get to the drop-off point. Some artists opted to use area parking lots and carry their critters instead. All were relieved when their dogs were inside the building and going through Downtown Racine Corporation's check-in process.

Some artists were just happy to have delivered their dogs. Others bid their creative canines fond

Scott Bullock unloads Laughing Dog *from the back of his pick-up truck.*

and even somewhat sad farewells. As Louise (Sliv) Kasen reported, "I will miss *Diana*. She has been the perfect dog. The visiting granddogs are indifferent to her but my cat Bandit is proud to be a model."

Many of the artists spent a few minutes looking at the other works of art already checked in. They marveled at the creative efforts of their peers. They shared stories of trials and tribulations and learned they weren't the only ones who faced challenges.

And at the end of the day April 16, the special kennel for the Dog Days of Summer was packed, as the canine critters took up residence and awaited the next steps in their exciting journeys.

Dick Meinert walks close to the construction barricade fence as he delivers Mirror Mirror on the Dog, *one of the canines created by his daughter, Krista Lea Meinert Edquist.*

Left: *The dog delivery sign helps guide Dorothy Smalancke and "Eyes"-Abel, the canine she and Jan Caretta created, through the construction site.*

Below: Golden Days of Summer, *the complete vignette created by Philip Krejcarek of Dousman, Wisconsin, is so heavy it requires the muscle power of four people.*

Right: *Downtown Racine Corporation's Kathy Hansen and* Journal Times *photographer Gregory Shaver admire* Good Buoy, *created by Barb Henley.*

Below: *Kathy Hansen checks in Trenton Baylor and his K-9-3756.*

Above: Sandy Schmitz delivers Ain't Nothin' but a Hound Dog.

Left: Linden Schulz delivers his decorative ornamental metal bench creation, Dog Bone.

From 1848 to Today— and into the Future

Monument Square is in the heart of Downtown Racine, on Main Street between Fifth and Sixth streets. The new Racine Art Museum, scheduled to open in 2003, will be housed in the building shown at the right.

Downtown Racine hugs the shore of Lake Michigan, about 30 miles south of Milwaukee and 80 miles north of Chicago. It was the start of a city founded in 1848.

Through the years, Racine enjoyed tremendous growth as an industrial and residential complex, with Downtown providing its significant mercantile and social center.

Downtown Racine in the late 1970s and early 1980s experienced what so many other downtown areas, especially those in the industrialized Midwest, endured—the flight to the outlying areas. Before long, Downtown Racine was plagued by empty storefronts, inertia and general lack of interest and activity.

Thanks to the leadership and forward thinking of area business people and residents, the Downtown's plight was soon addressed and Downtown Racine Development Corporation, predecessor to today's Downtown Racine Corporation, was born. The organization went to work.

"We had a lot of work to do," said Brian Anderson, today's chairman of the board of directors of Downtown Racine Corporation, "but we

Downtown Racine is bordered on the east by Lake Michigan. Highlights in this panorama include Festival Hall and Park, with the new Johnson Building in the center.

knew if we worked hard together we could make things happen." Anderson has been active Downtown since the early 1980s.

"When you look at Downtown today and compare it with the early '80s, there's very little comparison. We've come a long way in returning Downtown to its position as a significant destination for our community," Anderson said.

Festival Hall and Park were built on Lake Michigan's shore. A new marina was developed. New housing—in the form of apartments, condominiums and townhouses—sprang up Downtown.

New businesses started moving in.

As the upturn gained momentum, an annual black-tie fund raiser was started. Originally called Renaissance Ball, the first two events were held in tents, one on a farm on the outskirts of town and the second right Downtown. The weather was cold but people didn't seem to mind. They enjoyed evenings of sharing the successes that were starting to happen in Downtown Racine.

When Festival Hall was completed in November of 1987, the events had a new home they used for several years as the fund raiser continued.

The Root River forms Downtown Racine's border on North Main Street.

The city's harbor on the east side of Downtown Racine was developed in the '80s as the area began its modern-day renaissance.

As years progressed, there were periods where it looked as though Downtown Racine was again stagnating. And then it would swing upward. And each year the fund-raising gala was held. Its named changed to Boathouse Ball, in honor of the value of the marinas to the Downtown community.

Today, Downtown is flourishing. This city of more than 81,000 people once again has a Downtown center that has much to offer.

"The current Downtown plan being implemented is the first plan which had the input of the community and was adopted by the Racine City Council as the land use plan for Downtown," Anderson said. "I think our new successes Downtown are because of this plan and having new great projects like One Main Centre and the Johnson Building, both which have had great spin-off effects."

Putting on the Dog

This year the Downtown Racine Corporation annual fundraiser paid tribute to the Dog Days of Summer. Held May 4 in the new Johnson Building at 555 Main Street, Putting on the Dog was the first public showing of the 149 dogs that would decorate Downtown's Main and Sixth streets until October. It was here that the 150th canine, dubbed *Naked Dog*, was auctioned off to the highest bidder.

It was here that people came together to celebrate

Above: *Downtown Racine Corporation Chairman Brian Anderson poses with* Meowzer, *created by Franklin Deracin.*

Left: *Debra and Russ Weyers served as co-chairs for Putting on the Dog.*

Below: *Gene and Sam Johnson discuss the details on* El Dia del Perro Muerto, *created by Alex Mandli, Jr.*

Downtown Racine, knowing full well they had much to celebrate while anticipating much more to do in the future—to make sure Downtown Racine continued its development as a final exciting, vibrant destination for residents and visitors alike.

"When anything is worth doing, it's worth doing well," Anderson said. "Our Dog Days of Summer is one of the best events we've ever held Downtown. It shows what a community can do when it gets a good idea and then involves hundreds of people to make it happen."

Above: Kathy Hansen presents Gene Johnson with a thank-you gift for all of Johnson's work on Dog Days of Summer.

Below: Richard Hansen, president of Johnson International, and Kathy Hansen, executive director of Downtown Racine Corporation, are totally ignored by "Pup"Lo Picasso, created by Jenny Pelton.

Solomon, owned by B.J. Wilcox, was one of a dozen real live dogs who greeted guests at Putting on the Dog. All are members of the Greater Racine Kennel Club.

Above: *County Executive Jean Jacobson and husband Phil get no attention from Edgar Dogas, created by Tanya Fuhrman.*

Below: *Mayor Jim Smith and* Journal Times *publisher Richard Johnston discuss exciting activities happening in Downtown Racine.*

Bruce Pepich and Lisa Englander of Wustum Museum of Fine Arts and Racine Art Museum use Linden Schulz's Dog Bone *for its intended purpose—as a bench.*

The Dogs Go on Display

Dogs await their assignments on Main and Sixth streets in Downtown Racine. They are on display from May through early October.

The dogs hit Downtown streets starting Tuesday, May 7, as they began appearing in storefront windows.

The dogs are in a concentrated area—on Main Street from the Root River south to Sixth Street, and on Sixth Street west to Grand Avenue, which makes an easy walk for the viewer.

Fifty of the dogs are on pull carts so they spend their days outdoors. The rest are on exhibit in storefront and business windows, so they're easy to see and enjoy.

Dog Days of Summer officially ends Sunday afternoon, October 13, at an artists' party and auction, with festivities held under a large canopy covering the half-block-square area at the corner of State and Main streets. At that time, the artists are honored and their dogs sold at auction.

The auction's proceeds are shared equally by Downtown Racine Corporation and Racine Art Museum.

The following 11 sections profile the artists, show their dogs and list their dogs' sponsors, in addition to the dogs discussed earlier in this book.

Above: Naked Dog *maintained a four-months-long vigil at the Downtown Racine Corporation Main Street office while his 149 associates underwent their artistic transformations.* Naked Dog *went to his new home May 4, following the auction at Putting on the Dog, while his compatriots went on exhibit starting May 7, for their five-month public art display.*

Left (top): *When the need for pull carts for the dogs became apparent, the staff at Grainger Industrial Supply encouraged Branch Manager Amy Rose-Offord (right) to donate 50 carts to the project. Community volunteer Mike Miklasevich, owner of Double M Investments (left) and his associates assembled and painted the carts, then installed the dogs on them, as he's shown doing with Hard-ly.*

Left (bottom): *Terrance Bendrin and Bruce Meekma of Seater Construction carry canines to various Downtown business establishments.*

Right *Children of all ages are fascinated with the creative Labradors lining Main and Sixth streets.*

Below: *Decorated Labs welcome Downtown visitors in Racine's first-ever Downtown public art event.*

Arts & Entertainment

Arts and entertainment provided plenty of material for the artists who designed the 24 Labradors shown in this section and the critters profiled in Cows/Dogs, Chicago/Racine and The Dogs Who Came from School. Here one will find everything from comic-book characters to critters inspired by masters such as Pablo Picasso and Vincent van Gogh.

"Dogs love company. They place it first in their short list of needs."

—J. R. Ackerley

Ain't Nothin' but a Hound Dog

Artists: Sandy Schmitz, Mary Ann Logic and friends, Racine

This tribute to Elvis Presley was created by Sandy Schmitz, proprietor, The Cobblestone Ltd., professional framer and three-dimensional artist; Mary Ann Logic, designer, printmaker, two-dimensional artist; and the dedicated help of special family and friends: Ron Brankey, Bill Saunders and Laverne VanDerZee.

Sponsor: The Cobblestone, Ltd.

Aletta 4U

Artist: William F. Hinca, Racine

William Hinca has been involved in the sign and graphic field for 24 years. He and his work have been profiled in several graphic publications. His fields of expression include designing, drawing, painting, woodworking and metallurgical media. He has taught classes at Waukesha County Technical College.

Sponsor: Bank of Elmwood

Patches

Artist: Sue Causey, Racine

Patches is a natural extension of Sue Causey's passion for quilting. Causey is a full-time real estate broker who pursues her creative endeavors, including papermaking as well as quilting, in her spare time. Assisting with Patches were Terri Sharp, Hannah Wosilait, Lori Destiche and Linda Schubring, Causey's associates at Coldwell Banker Residential Brokerage.

Sponsor: Sue Causey

Deco Dasha—Divine Display

Artists: Terri Ann Fox, Franksville, and Tonya Lambeth Dilley, Racine

Terri Ann Fox owns a small business, Foxden Designs, centered on specialized beadwork and jewelry design and fabrication. Her background includes architectural interior design and drafting. Tonya Lambeth Dilley holds her bachelor of fine arts from University of Wisconsin–Parkside. Her recent creative endeavors include ornamental garden planning, furniture embellishments, personal artwork, and the occasional crayon project with her young son.

Sponsor: Foxden Designs

Salvador Dogi

Artist: Jeffrey D. Shawhan, Racine

Jeffrey D. Shawhan has his bachelor of arts degree from the University of Wisconsin–Parkside and his master of fine arts degree in ceramics from the University of Wisconsin–Milwaukee. He currently is an assistant professor of art at Concordia University, Milwaukee. His works are shown in various galleries and collections throughout the United States.

Sponsor: Garbo Motor Sales, Inc.

The Wizard of Dogz

Artist: Jayne Miner, Racine

Jayne Miner has been an art teacher for Racine Unified schools the past 23 years. She currently teaches at Case High School. She has her bachelor of arts degree from Calvin College and her master's degree in education from Carthage College. Miner enjoys designing and creating watercolor paintings, stained glass and art metals.

Sponsor: Gateway Technical College/Racine—Student Services

Batdog and Robin

Artists: Paul Georgeson and Kelly Galbraith, Menomonie, Wisconsin

Both Paul Georgeson and Kelly Galbraith are juniors at the University of Wisconsin–Stout. Georgeson is working on his bachelor of arts degree with a concentration in industrial design, while Galbraith is working on her BA degree with a concentration in graphic design. Georgeson is a Racine native, and Galbraith is from Burnsville, Minnesota.

Sponsors: John and Cynthia Georgeson

Bowzer

Artist: Conor Lalor, Racine

A 16-year-old student at Horlick High School, Conor Lalor has been drawing all his life. He has taken art classes at Spectrum and at Horlick. Art is a serious consideration for his profession in the future.

Sponsor: Ron Jones

"Eyes" Abel

Artists: Jan Caretta and Dorothy Smalancke, Racine

Both Jan Caretta and Dorothy Smalancke are members of the National Society of Decorative Painters and the Wisconsin chapter, Turp 'n Stein. Both have studied with local and national artists. Smalancke has been doing decorative painting for more than 20 years and Caretta has been exhibiting at craft shows the past 14 years. Smalancke paints in oils and acrylics, while Caretta's preferred medium is oils.

Sponsor: Linda DuVall

Evolution of the Species

Artist: Robert Michelson, Racine

Born in St. Louis, Robert Michelson studied at Beloit College, University College of North Wales in the United Kingdom, and received his law degree from Duke University. He served as municipal judge for the City of Racine from 1974 to 2002 and has practiced law here since 1972.

Sponsor: Michelson Law Office

"Pup"Lo Picasso

Artist: Jenny Pelton, Racine

A Racine native, Jenny Pelton graduated from the University of Wisconsin–Madison with a degree in advertising. She owned her own graphic design business for several years and currently works at Renquist/Associates, Inc., as a senior graphic designer.

Sponsor: Renquist/Associates, Inc.

Justice

Artists: Domenica Zanni and Sean Schoettler, Racine

Domenica Zanni and Sean Schoettler, both graphic artists, have been working for *The Journal Times* for three and four-and-one-half years respectively. Through the years they have collaborated on several projects for *The Journal Times*. The idea for their dog stemmed from their mutual childhood memories of watching the "Justice League of America" cartoon series.

Sponsor: *The Journal Times*

Porcelain Pooch

Artist: Anne Meredith, Racine

Anne Meredith, a Racine native, has her bachelor of arts degree in studio arts/languages from the University of Minnesota. She spent 10 years abroad in the travel industry. She currently is employed as a regional account executive selling direct mail marketing/advertising. She is a freelance artist/painter in her free time.

Sponsor: Maresh-Meredith & Acklam Funeral Home

The Labrador of Lilliput

Artist: Melanie Pope, Racine

Melanie Pope is a senior at the University of Wisconsin–Whitewater, majoring in fine arts with an emphasis on drawing and painting. She accepts commissions for art projects, such as murals in businesses and homes, including the Racine Public Library's story room. She works mainly with acrylic or oil paint and charcoal, and looks forward to illustrating children's books some day.

Sponsor: Racine Public Library

Springer

Artist: Caitlin Pond, Racine

A junior at Horlick High School, Caitlin Pond is a high honors student. She is president of Key Club and on Horlick's girls' tennis team and yearbook staff. She enjoys arts and crafts and has excelled in them both in and out of school. She hopes to attend the University of Minnesota and study to become a children's dentist.

Sponsor: Vista Dental

Jack the Dripper: A Tribute to Jackson Pollock

Artist: Robert W. Andersen, Racine

A Racine native, Robert Andersen has been an art teacher in the Racine Unified School District for 29 years and an active local artist for three decades. A graduate of Park High School, he received his bachelor of science degree in art from the University of Wisconsin–Whitewater and his master's degree in education from Carthage College.

Sponsor: Sustainable Racine

Crescendo

Artist: Todd C. Dwyer, Racine

A professional structures (not art) painter, Todd Dwyer graduated from Case High School and did his painting apprenticeship at Gateway Technical College. Crescendo is his first venture into the fine arts. He wanted to do something new and more challenging so he created the dog.

Sponsor: Harborfest, Inc.

SpiderRAM

Artist: Ima LaBrador and Talz A. Waggin

This nimble canine, created by the new Racine Art Museum (RAM), calls attention to the museum's grand opening in Downtown Racine in spring 2003. It will present one of the most significant collections of contemporary crafts of any North American art museum. The newly renovated facility—an effort worthy of a superhero—will include a museum store, art library and exciting public places.

Sponsor: Anonymous

Flower Pup

Artists: Sally Orth, Franksville, and Terry Leopold, Racine

Both Sally Orth and Terry Leopold are former teachers, Orth with a degree from the University of Wisconsin–Oshkosh and Leopold with a degree from Otterbein College in Westerville, Ohio. They are active in community work in the Racine area and during the past several years have collaborated on a variety of volunteer projects.

Sponsor: Washington Properties, Inc.

Vincent Van Dog

Artist: Jay Harris, Waterford, Wisconsin

Jay Harris works as a graphic designer in Downtown Racine. He graduated from Northern Illinois University with a bachelor's degree in art and a master's degree in philosophy. While in school he worked in any medium possible. He prefers sketching in pastels, and acrylics and he continues to draw and paint when not playing guitar in a band.

Sponsor: Design Partners, Inc.

Vinney

Artist: Kathryn Gagliardi, Brighton, Wisconsin

A University of Wisconsin–Parkside graduate with a bachelor's degee in art, Kathryn Gagliardi teaches art at St. Joseph High School in Kenosha. She has exhibited in the area for several years, including shows at Anderson Gallery, Lemon St. Gallery and Gallery 124 in Kenosha, and Wustum Museum of Fine Arts and Spectrum in Racine.

Sponsor: Jim and Deanna Parrish

Edgar "Dogas"

Artist: Tanya Fuhrman, Waterford, Wisconsin

Tanya Fuhrman studied art at the University of Wisconsin–Whitewater and University of Wisconsin–Milwaukee. A special education aide with autistic children in the Racine public schools, she has painted murals for churches, businesses and private homes. She also has designed and constructed stained glass artwork.

Sponsor: Avenue Frame Shop

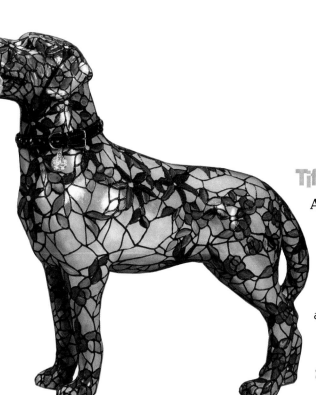

Tiffany

Artist: Lori Schory, Genoa City, Wisconsin

Lori Schory, a Chicago native, has her master of fine arts degree from Northern Illinois University. Since 1983 she has been specializing in custom hand lettering and graphics for boats, vans, trucks and signage of all types. She accepts individual commissions for pictorial murals and hand-painted accessories and furniture to coordinate with any environment.

Sponsor: Faye Becker Homes, Inc.

Fashion

Fashion comes in many forms and makes a variety of statements in the process. These 15 critters run the gamut from punk to high fashion.

"A dog is the only thing on earth that loves you more than you love yourself."

—Josh Billings

Carmen the Star of CopaLABana

Artists: Pat Levine, Racine, and Rebekah Levine, Chicago

Pat Levine and daughter Rebekah Levine have major artistic achievements to their credit. Pat Levine is a professional interior designer who has won national design awards. She is a professional member of the American Society of Interior Designers. Rebekah Levine received her bachelor of fine arts degree from the School of the Art Institute of Chicago, where she begins her master's program in modern art history in September 2002. Her preferred media are photography and video. Her works have been exhibited throughout the United States and in Mexico.

Sponsor: Water's Edge Clothiers

Lady and the Tramp

Artist: Sarah Nahikian, Racine

Racine native Sarah Nahikian is a graduate of The Prairie School and in fall 2002 will attend Skidmore College, where she hopes to major in art, English or drama. In addition to painting and theater, Sarah loves to dance and is looking forward to studying that in college also.

Sponsor: Norco Manufacturing Corporation

A Fetching Dog

Artist: Nancy J. Greenebaum, Racine

Racine artist Nancy Greenebaum was trained at the School of the Museum of Fine Arts in Boston, and the University of Wisconsin–Milwaukee, where she received her fine arts master's degree. Her works have been widely exhibited and internationally collected. She is a member of Artists' Gallery on Sixth Street in Racine.

Sponsor: Sue's Yarn Basket/dba The Serendipity Shoppe

Delhi Dog

Artist: Darrin Neuschaefer, Racine

Darrin Neuschaefer has had a life-long passion for the arts and has studied interior design. He has worked as a floral artist for several years and has extensive experience in the restaurant business. He currently operates his own painting business with focus on fine painted furniture.

Sponsor: Dimple's Fine Imports

68

Poochi 2002

Artist: Tammy Woolrage, Racine

Tammy Woolrage has an associate degree in commercial art from Milwaukee Area Technical College. For the past 20 years she has created hand-made resin pieces and used them for jewelry and on clothing. She has participated in a number of Wisconsin art and fashion shows, and she now is also working in graphic design and marketing.

Sponsor: Eye Centers of Racine and Kenosha

Lab-adore

Artist: Sonia Buchaklian, Racine

Sonia Buchaklian is a graduate of Horlick High School and the University of Wisconsin–Madison. She has been a teacher, floral designer, manager of a hospital gift shop and presently sells "baubles" at a Racine jewelry store. Creating Lab-adore has been a fun project because she enjoys things that are whimsical.

Sponsor: Adecco

Rin Tin Tin

Artist: Greg Helding, Racine

Greg Helding became interested in drawing in grade school and was an A student in high school art classes. Twenty years later, he started taking night classes at Wustum Museum of Fine Arts in Racine. Since then, his works have appeared in a number of regional juried exhibitions. His usual medium is two-dimensional pastel on paper.

Sponsor: Joan Celeste

Pink Poochy

Artist: Sarah Prince Frey, Milwaukee

Sarah Prince Frey graduated from the Milwaukee Institute of Art and Design as a drawing major in 1991. She then worked as assistant director for continuing education at MIAD for 10 years. Currently a stay-at-home mom, she enjoys painting colorful abstract compositions and also enjoys computer design, including Web sites.

Sponsor: Martinizing Dry Cleaning

Reflections

Artist: Tanya Fuhrman, Waterford, Wisconsin

Tanya Fuhrman studied art at the University of Wisconsin–Whitewater and University of Wisconsin–Milwaukee. A special education aide with autistic children in the Racine public schools, she has painted murals for churches, businesses and private homes. She also has designed and constructed stained glass artwork.

Sponsor: SC Johnson

Tiedo

Artist: Ellen Gutknecht, Franksville, Wisconsin

Ellen Gutknecht, with a bachelor's degree in art education from Eastern Kentucky University and an associate degree in interior design from Gateway Technical College, teaches art to kindergartners through third graders at Salem Grade School. She is currently working on her master's degree in teacher leadership at Silver Lake College, Manitowoc.

Sponsor: Anastasia and Garrison Priem

Sid Vicious

Artists: Sylwia Mataczynski and Greg Francis, Racine

Both Sylwia Mataczynski and Greg Francis are seniors at Case High School, Racine, and are both punk rock enthusiasts. They hope their dog eliminates the stereotype of punks being lazy and nothing but trouble, but rather as people who contribute to the diversity of the community. Both are members of the National Honor Society and participate in a variety of extra-curricular activities.

Sponsor: Norm Monson

Hot Dog

Artist: Brooke Walker, Racine

A fine arts degree has provided the opportunity for lots of fun for Brooke Walker. She does freelance projects like furniture painting, home accessories and needlepoint canvases for family and friends. In the past, she did newspaper fashion ads for a large Milwaukee department store.

Sponsor: Jensen Metal Products

Perro de Colores

Artist: Jo Anne Wood, Racine

A lifelong Racine resident, Jo Anne Wood has a degree in art education from the University of Wisconsin–Madison. A former middle school art teacher and children's book editor, Wood is currently co-owner and creative director for *Copycat*, a national magazine for K-3 teachers.

Sponsor: WISPARK LLC

Mirror Mirror on the Dog

Artist: Krista Lea Meinert Edquist, Racine

Shortly after Krista Lea Meinert Edquist received her fine arts degree from the University of Wisconsin–Parkside in 1998, she was commissioned to design the layout for a compact disk project, followed by other work, including a mural for a multi-million-dollar corporation. In 2002 her photographs and sculptures were accepted for Wustum Museum of Fine Arts' Tri-County Photographic Print Competition and Racine Area Arts Exhibition.

Sponsor: TDS Metrocom

Dazzle Dog

Artist: Deirdre Lapinski, Racine

Deirdre Lapinski has a bachelor of science degree in nursing from the University of Wisconsin–Milwaukee. Art has always been part of her life, and sewing has been her primary medium. She began beading activities about three years ago and that now continues to occupy her free time.

Sponsor: Nordik of America

Leisure-Time Pursuits

There's so much people can do with their leisure time—from enjoying a culinary treat to playing with toys. These 19 dogs and the critters shown in The Dogs Come from School touch on some of the leisure-time opportunities one pursues.

"I always find it endearing when a Labrador, that most mature and dignified of breeds on the surface, reveals the puppyishness which is never far beneath."

—Gerald Hammond

75

Buddy

Artist: George R. Zielinski, Waukesha, Wisconsin

George Zielinski has been a watercolor artist for nearly 30 years. A Vietnam veteran, he specializes in aviation art and is commissioned on a regular basis. A self-taught artist, Zielinski has exhibited his works in the Waukesha area and in Door County. He enjoys working in watercolors and pastels. This is his first venture into three-dimensional work.

Sponsor: Flowers by Walter

Dog and Suds

Artist: LeeAnn Morelli, Racine

LeeAnn Morelli has been a commercial artist and graphic designer for more than 25 years, 16 of which have been with Case Corporation. A life-long resident of Racine, she is a graduate of Layton School of Art, Milwaukee. Morelli, a devoted animal lover, does commissioned portraits for individuals and organizations, in addition to her commercial work.

Sponsor: CNH/Case Corporation

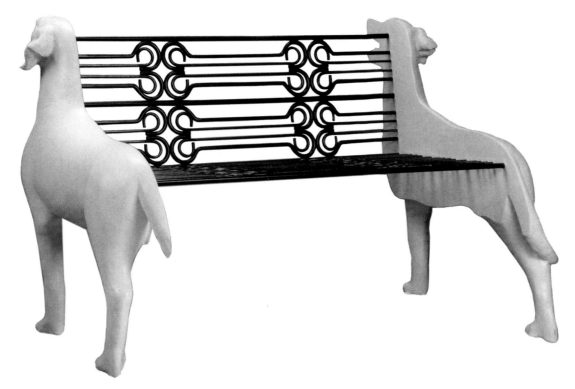

Dog Bone

Artist: Linden Schulz, Racine

Linden Schulz owns L.A.S. Sculpturewerks, a Racine business that focuses on the production and restoration of sculpture, ornamental metal and decorative arts. He received his bachelor of fine arts degree in sculpture from the University of Wisconsin–Milwaukee with a primary focus on bronze casting. Prior to opening his own studio he worked as a studio artist for several firms.

Sponsor: Inspec, Inc.

Chili Dawg

Artist: Pat King, Milwaukee

An art teacher at Shorewood High School, Pat King has been involved in the arts for 37 years. She currently has two paintings on exhibit at Watercolor Wisconsin at Wustum Museum of Fine Arts. She loves both painting and sculpture and enjoys combining the two. She also conducts critiques for local art societies and gives painting demonstrations.

Sponsor: Robert W. Baird

K9

Artist: Jane Hobbs-Cascio, Racine

Jane Hobbs-Cascio received a bachelor's degree in fine arts from Rockford College. She currently teaches at Wustum Museum of Fine Arts, Creative Learning Montessori in Barrington, Illinois, and for Main Gallery. She is an active member of the Artists' Gallery and has shown her works in several area juried shows, including Racine Area Arts and Watercolor Wisconsin.

Sponsor: Dover Flag and Map

Carousel K-9

Artist: Kelly Drumm, Racine

Kelly Drumm, a Horlick High School honor student who graduated in June 2002, will attend the University of Wisconsin-Milwaukee, majoring in journalism and minoring in art. She spent two summers working as a young artist within the Racine Parks, Recreational and Cultural Department's Main Gallery, where her pieces raised money at the charity auctions held at summer's end.

Sponsor: Johnson Bank

Gus—Goes to the Beach

Artist: Kevin Pearson, Franksville

Kevin Pearson grew up in Moline, Illinois, and graduated from Augustana College. After an apprenticeship in clay, he operated a pottery studio in Egg Harbor, Wisconsin, for 10 years. Pearson has been at The Prairie School in Racine for the past 22 years as a teacher or administrator. He currently is the head of the art department.

Sponsor: Karen and Sara Johnson

79

Bonne a la Bone

Artist: Bill Reid, Racine

Nationally known sculptor Bill Reid received his bachelor of fine arts degree from Kansas City (Missouri) Art Institute and his master's degree in fine arts from Cranbook Academy of Art in Bloomfield Hills, Michigan. A graduate of The Prairie School, Racine, he also studied at Lawrence University in Appleton and in its program in London, England.

Sponsor: Samuel and Gene Johnson

Gardenia

Artist: Amber Schemenauer, Racine

A Racine native, Amber Schemenauer is a senior at Horlick High School. She is interested in many areas of the arts, including sculpting, painting, drawing and drama. She has expressed a desire to pursue her interests in fashion and fashion design by one day owning her own boutique and perhaps creating a line of her own couture.

Sponsor: Out of the Pan Café and Catering

 80

Sam E. Dog, Adventurer

Artist: Ada M. James, Racine

A graduate of the University of Northern Colorado, Ada James had private shows in Colorado, Wyoming and Winnetka, Illinois. Her work has been published in journals, magazines, and advertising and promotional pieces. In 1998, she was commissioned by the National Spiritual Assembly of the Baha'is of the United States to complete a drawing on the theme of Women and Peace.

Sponsor: Gorman and Company, Inc.

Chocolate Lab with Sprinkles, Whipped Cream, on a Waffle Cone with a Cherry on Top

Artists: Dick Huennekens, Racine, and Mike Phillips, Milwaukee

A graphic design professional, Dick Huennekens enjoys arts, architecture, Wisconsin outdoors and family events. A long-time Racine resident, he is a graduate of Layton School of Art. Mike Phillips is an industrial design graduate of Milwaukee Institute of Art and Design. Originally from Syracuse, New York, Mike is a photographer and an avid competitive bicycle racer.

Sponsor: Chocolate Fest

81

Bath Time

Artist: Krista Lea Meinert Edquist, Racine

Shortly after Krista Lea Meinert Edquist received her fine arts degree from the University of Wisconsin–Parkside in 1998, she was commissioned to design the layout for a compact disk project, followed by other work, including a mural for a multi-million-dollar corporation. In 2002 her photographs and sculptures were acceptcd for Wustum Museum of Fine Arts' Tri-County Photographic Print Competition and Racine Area Arts Exhibition.

Sponsor: All Saints Healthcare

Flea Circus

Artists: Jodi Soczka and Amy Soczka, Racine

Sisters Jodi and Amy Soczka have loved and studied art since they could hold a crayon. Jodi graduated from the University of Wisconsin–Parkside with a bachelor of arts degree in fine art and is currently is a member of the Lemon Street Gallery in Kenosha. Amy is a graphic design student at Milwaukee Institute of Art and Design.

Sponsor: Beth Truax

Dog Dreams

Artist: Marian J. Kane, Prairie du Sac, Wisconsin

Marian Kane, a professional artist and primarily a painter, is a graduate of the School of Art Institute of Chicago, her native city. Her work is typically representational and involved with themes of perception, expectation and emotion. Her work has been shown at the Art Institute of Chicago, the Madison Art Center and the Milwaukee Art Museum.

Sponsor: Racine Veterinary Hospital

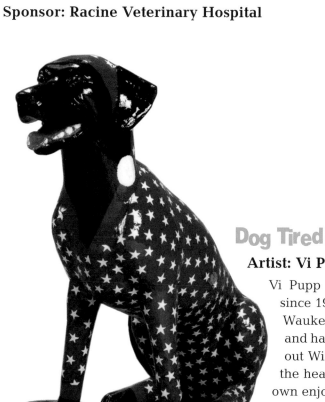

Dog Tired

Artist: Vi Pupp Scroggins, Watertown, Wisconsin

Vi Pupp Scroggins has worked in oil and watercolor since 1967. She taught continuing education classes at Waukesha County Technical College for many years and has been a ribbon winner at many shows throughout Wisconsin. She currently is a design consultant in the health care market. She sculpts and paints for her own enjoyment at this time.

Sponsor: Beechwood Veterinary Clinic

Photo-Lab

Artist: Dick Huennekens, Racine

A graphic design professional, Dick Huennekens enjoys the arts, architecture, Wisconsin outdoors and family events. A long-time Racine resident, he is a graduate of Layton School of Art, Milwaukee.

Sponsor: Camera World

Birthday Baby

Artist: Susan M. Edgerton, Milwaukee

Susan M. Edgerton, a Racine native, received her bachelor of arts degree from the University of Wisconsin–Parkside. She is a founding member of Lemon Street Gallery in Kenosha and has had her works displayed in Wisconsin galleries, exhibitions and shops. She also has done illustration and design for Wisconsin companies and publications, and her writing has appeared in several periodicals.

Sponsor: Donald and Gabriella Klein

Toy Hound

Artist: Franklin Deracin, Racine

A native of Racine, Franklin Deracin has taken a variety of art courses at the University of Wisconsin–Milwaukee and University of Wisconsin–Parkside, and a computer illustration class at Gateway Technical College. He works in several media and enjoys combining sculpture and painting, with his creations giving the impression of one thing but upon closer look revealing something quite different.

Sponsor: Shear Madness

Santa's Lab

Artist: Chuck Torosian, Racine

Racine native Chuck Torosian was an art director and illustrator for leading advertising agencies in Chicago, New York and Los Angeles. Now semi-retired, he is active in the fine arts community. He teaches fine arts and marketing, creates advertising and develops artwork concepts for children's books.

Sponsor: D. J. Kontra, M.D. and Associates, S.C.

Other Critters

A dog as a cat? A bug ball? How about butter-flies? A Labrador friendly to the likes of cats and other critters? All are found here among these 21 creative canines, as well as in the article The Dogs Come from School.

"To call him a dog hardly seems to do him justice, though inasmuch as he had four legs, a tail and barked, I admit he was, to all outward appearances. But to those of us who knew him well, he was a perfect gentleman."

—Hermione Gingold

Bird Dog

Artist: Kate Smallish, Saukville, Wisconsin

A professional artist, Kate Smallish has had her own studio for more than 25 years. She works and teaches in oils, pastels and watercolor. A lifelong Wisconsin resident, her work is representational. She draws upon strong colors and contrasts in depicting the Wisconsin landscape. She also does art restoration. Her works appear in many public and private collections internationally.

Sponsor: CRB Insurance

Bow Wow Cow

Artist: Penelope Grill, New York City and Racine

Penelope (Penny) Grill, a fine artist, graphic and Web designer, divides her time between New York and Wisconsin. A graduate of Washington Park High School, Racine, and Hollins University in Virginia, she also attended graduate school at American University in Washington, DC. Her works have been shown in a number of exhibits in New York.

Sponsor: SC Johnson

Anemone

Artist: Kurt Erdman, Racine

Kurt Erdman, who has lived in Southeastern Wisconsin his entire life, graduated from the University of Wisconsin–Parkside with a bachelor's degree in art. He has not made any long-term career decisions yet. He had several pieces accepted into UW–Parkside gallery shows and won Best in Show at the 1999 student exhibit with a large welded-steel sculpture.

Sponsor: Norm Monson

Rip—The Bird Dog

Artist: Cary Hunkel, Madison, Wisconsin

Cary Hunkel was educated at the University of Wisconsin–Madison where she earned her master of fine arts degree. She is a member of the Society of Animal Artists, and her watercolors and drawings have been shown throughout North America. She also has illustrated several wildlife books and articles. Her two active retrievers inspired her license plate—K9 KAOS.

Sponsor: Racine Gymnastics Center and Peppermint Preschool Gymnastics

Racine Dog Disguised as a Chicago Cow

Artist: Gary Wolfe, Racine

An interior designer who specializes in restaurant design, Gary Wolfe was born in Virginia and has lived in Wisconsin since 1986. He recently moved his design studio from Milwaukee to West Sixth Street in Racine.

Sponsor: Knight-Barry Title, Inc.

Chicken-Poodle Soup

Artist: Judy Olsen-Yorgan, Racine

Judy Olsen-Yorgan is the owner, designer and goldsmith of Plumb Gold Ltd., in Downtown Racine since 1976. Among her local commissions are works for University of Wisconsin–Parkside, Carthage College, Case-Tenneco Corporation, Unico and The Prairie School. Daughter Valerie Yorgan conceived the concept for this dog, based on Haskins, a standard poodle and family pet for 16 years.

Sponsor: Plumb Gold Ltd.

Hakuna Mutt Tata

Artist: Sue Horton, Franksville, Wisconsin

A Chicago native, Sue Horton earned a bachelor of science degree in nursing from Loyola University of Chicago. After residing in Dusseldorf, Germany, for three years because of her husband's job assignment, she became a full-time homemaker and devotes time to her art. Recent projects include murals, school play sets, painting ceramic tiles and bisqueware and drawing landscapes and portraits.

Sponsor: The Horton Family

Meowzer

Artist: Franklin Deracin, Racine

A native of Racine, Franklin Deracin has taken a variety of art courses at the University of Wisconsin–Milwaukee and University of Wisconsin–Parkside, and a computer illustration class at Gateway Technical College. He works in several media and enjoys combining sculpture and painting, with his creations giving the impression of one thing but upon closer look revealing something quite different.

Sponsor: Porters of Racine

Trojan Dog

Artist: Renee Staeck, Milwaukee

Racine native Renee Staeck is a senior drawing major at Milwaukee Institute of Art and Design. She enjoys painting, drawing and making sculpture for commission work and as a personal outlet. She has done projects for many clients in the Racine area, and has exhibited her work in Milwaukee galleries and the John Michael Kohler Arts Center in Sheboygan.

Sponsor: Landmark Title of Racine, Inc.

Darwin's Animal Pajamas

Artist: Lisa Dukowitz, Kenosha

Lisa Dukowitz earned a master's degree in fine arts in painting and drawing from the University of Wisconsin–Milwaukee and is currently instructing courses for Carthage College and St. Edward's Elementary School in Racine. Her landscape paintings have been exhibited nationally since 1998. She keeps inspired by exploring Great Lakes islands via sea kayak and teaching children about the importance of wildlife preservation.

Sponsor: Racine Zoological Society

Puppy Tut

Artist: Kate Smallish, Saukville, Wisconsin

A professional artist, Kate Smallish has had her own studio for more than 25 years. She works and teaches in oils, pastels and watercolor. A lifelong Wisconsin resident, her work is representational. She draws upon strong colors and contrasts in depicting the Wisconsin landscape. She also does art restoration. Her works appear in many public and private collections internationally.

Sponsor: Johnson Bank

Snuggle

Artist: Krista Lea Meinert Edquist, Racine

Shortly after Krista Lea Meinert Edquist received her fine arts degree from the University of Wisconsin–Parkside in 1998, she was commissioned to design the layout for a compact disk project, followed by other work, including a mural for a multi-million-dollar corporation. In 2002 her photographs and sculptures were accepted for Wustum Museum of Fine Arts' Tri-County Photographic Print Competition and Racine Area Arts Exhibition.

Sponsor: O & H Danish Bakery

Found Friends

Artist: Violet O'Dell, Racine

Violet O'Dell is a freelance artist working in various media, with a three-dimensional emphasis. Though mostly self-taught, she took courses at Wustum Museum of Fine Arts during her high school years. She also attended the University of Wisconsin–Parkside. Most of her works have been privately commissioned. She presently is establishing her own studio.

Sponsor: Countryside Humane Society

Cock-A-Doodle-Dog

Artist: Amy Zahalka, Wind Lake, Wisconsin

Amy Zahalka received her art degree from the University of Wisconsin–Madison. During the years she has worked in graphics and visual merchandising. Since returning to the Midwest, she earned her teaching certificate from the University of Wisconsin–Milwaukee and began teaching art in Racine. She has had one show in Milwaukee and recently illustrated a children's book.

Sponsor: Friends of Racine Heritage Museum

One Fish, Two Fish, Cat Fish... Dog Fish

Artist: Lara Kazarian, Racine

Lara Kazarian is a Racine-born artist who recently graduated from Columbia College in Chicago with a concentration in traditional animation. She is seeking a position in her field of study while embarking on various independent projects.

Sponsor: Yardarm Bar and Grill

Raider

Artist: Peg Ducommun, Racine

Growing up in Antioch, Illinois, Peg Ducommun showed artistic talent at a young age. At 14 she began winning art contests and at 16 enjoyed freelancing for private homes. In the 1980s she entered her first juried competition. In March 2001 she held her first show. Currently she is creating wall art for the Waxdale plant in Sturtevant.

Sponsor: SC Johnson-Waxdale Aerosols

The Fancy Bug Ball

Artist: Sue Hollow, Racine

Currently a floral designer, Sue Hollow has had her artwork displayed in several shows at Wustum Museum of Fine Arts. Her most recent work was "You Decide," a black-and-white watercolor she painted the week following the September 11 tragedy. She has given out more than 700 prints in 26 states and seven countries.

Sponsor: Tom and Bonnie Prochaska

RAM's (Racine Art Museum) Best Friend

Artist: Ram Brandt van Rijn

After a year of ramming down walls and over-seeing construction demolition, this mascot, created by the new Racine Art Museum (RAM), celebrates the impending opening of the museum in Downtown Racine in 2003. With this project, the museum transforms a former mercantile structure into an exciting space devoted to exhibitions, including street-level pedestrian displays of artworks in storefront windows.

Sponsor: Karen and Bill Boyd

Barking Monarch

Artist: Sheryl A. Meyer, Racine

Currently a pre-school teacher, Sheryl Meyer enjoys using her artistic talent in the education of young children. She likes pencil sketching and working in charcoal. She recently completed a mural in her church. She is a self-taught artist who finds pleasure in painting with acrylics. She has received honors in art contests entered in the United States and Japan.

Sponsor: Dr. Robert and Sue Siegert

Lab-a-dabba-doo

Artist: Lois Van Liew, Thiensville, Wisconsin

Lois Van Liew holds a bachelor of art education degree from the University of Kansas in Lawrence, and has done advanced study at the University of Missouri (Kansas City campus) and Ox Bow in Saugatuck, Michigan. She has participated in many juried and invitational exhibits and won numerous awards for her work. Her works appear in many public and private collections.

Sponsor: Dr. and Mrs. Myron Mikaelian and Family

Butterfly Sky Dog

Artist: Jerry Belland, Racine

Jerry Belland has been a Racine area artist and teacher for more than 30 years. He has exhibited widely both regionally and nationally and represented Racine in the Aalborg, Denmark, Triennalle in the summer 2000. His work is part of the permanent collection at Wustum Museum of Fine Arts and his paintings hang in many public collections in Wisconsin.

Sponsor: SC Johnson

Outdoor Enjoyment

Labradors love the out of doors. And that love is what inspired the 10 dogs shown in this section. Smell the flowers; admire the trees; enjoy the seasons. All are here.

"If the history of all the dogs who have loved and been loved by the race of man could be written, each history of a dog would resemble all the other histories. It would be a love story."

—James Douglas

Daisy

Artist: Jeani Berndt, Burlington, Wisconsin

A freelance graphic designer, Jeani Berndt works in children's toys and publishing as well as advertising. She also teaches an after-school art program and an occasional college course. She enjoys the freedom of freelance, which allows her to spend most of her time with her husband and five children having fun on their farm.

Sponsor: Tenuta's Liquor and Deli

Little Dog on the Prairie

Artist: Mary Kuhnen, Caledonia, Wisconsin

Mary Kuhnen holds a bachelor's degree in fine arts from the University of Wisconsin–Madison. She has taught and practiced design for 20 years and is presently designing land-scapes. She also produces pastel drawings, mosaic garden furnishings and mixed media artwork.

Sponsor: Milaeger's, Inc.

99

Rag Doll

Artist: Susan M. Edgerton, Milwaukee

Susan M. Edgerton, a Racine native, received her bachelor of arts degree from the University of Wisconsin-Parkside. She is a founding member of Lemon Street Gallery in Kenosha and has had her works displayed in Wisconsin galleries, exhibitions and shops. She also has done illustration and design for Wisconsin companies and publications, and her writing has appeared in several periodicals.

Sponsor: WISPARK, LLC

Springer Spaniel

Artist: Christopher Dembroski, Milwaukee

A Racine native, Christopher Dembroski graduated from the Milwaukee Institute of Art and Design. He also has studied painting at the Studio Art Center International in Florence, Italy, and has been a guest at the Lacoste School of the Arts in Lacoste, France. He has worked in many art-related fields, from mural work to interior design.

Sponsor: E. C. Styberg Engineering Co.

Bou-K-9

Artists: Marie Skowronski and Cecilia Schmidt, Racine

Marie Skowronski and Cecilia Schmidt are sisters from a family of artists. Schmidt had art training when attending Dominican College, also art classes at Wustum Museum of Fine Arts and many art seminars. Skowronski had art classes while attending Horlick High School and classes at Wustum Museum of Fine Arts. They participate in local art events and paint with a seniors group at Chavez Center, Racine. For Bou-K-9, they pressed and dried flowers from their own gardens.

Sponsor: O'Neil Leather Specialties

Golden Days of Summer

Artist: Philip Krejcarek, Dousman, Wisconsin

A professor of art and co-chairman of the art department at Carroll College in Waukesha, Wisconsin, Philip Krejcarek has his master of fine arts degree from the University of Wisconsin–Milwaukee. He has exhibited at a number of shows around the United States and his works are included in several museums and private collections.

Sponsor: Mathis Gallery and Frame Shop

Bark

Artist: Jeff Levonian, Racine

Jeff Levonian graduated from University of Wisconsin–Parkside with a bachelor of arts degree in art. He uses art as a form of stress relief and enjoys sculpting and painting bulky or scaly animals, with elephants, rhinos and alligators being his favorites. Employed at Speedtech International, Inc., Levonian enjoys coaching soccer at Horlick High School.

Sponsor: Jay and Ric Ruffo

Provincial Labrador

Artist: Patricia A. Lenz, Maple, Wisconsin

Patricia Lenz is an avid collector of fragments—materials and ideas—which she recombines with paint in two- and three-dimensional collages. She has taught secondary and college art, been an arts administrator, and juried exhibits in the Upper Midwest. Her work has been included in national and international shows as well as private and public collections.

Sponsor: Twin Disc, Inc.

Afternoon in the Park

Artist: Deborah Bartelt, Oshkosh, Wisconsin

Deborah Bartelt graduated from the University of Wisconsin–Oshkosh with a bachelor of art degree in education. She received her master of science degree from St. Norbert College, DePere. A teacher in Oshkosh area schools, she focuses on the area of creativity for students, believing that creativity helps develop academic skills. Her personal growth has been in watercolor, drawing, paper making and photography.

Sponsor: Masters of Movement School of Dance

Copper

Artist: Stephanie Andersen, Racine

Currently working on a chemistry degree at the University of Wisconsin–Parkside, Stephanie Andersen has been involved in amateur photography for many years. Her favorite subject is Benjamin, her seven-year-old black Labrador. Andersen develops her own black-and-white prints in her basement darkroom and aspires to become an independent business owner.

Sponsor: Henricksen & Company, Inc.

Our Community

Community—a sense of togetherness, a tribute to all who live here, and actual scenes from Racine—all come together with the 13 canines in this section, as well as one in The Dogs Come from School.

"When the Man waked up he said, 'What is Wild Dog doing here?' And the Woman said, 'His name is not Wild Dog any more but First Friend, because he will be our friend for always and always and always.'"

—Rudyard Kipling

Ms. P. Gilbert

Artist: Linda M. Silvasi-Kelly, Baileys Harbor, Wisconsin

A Racine native who took childhood classes at Wustum Museum of Fine Arts, Linda Silvasi-Kelly has her bachelor of fine arts degree from the University of Wisconsin–Green Bay. A freelance artist, she works in several media. She has illustrated several books and designed ads, logos and brochures. She also does faux painting, trompe l'oeil and stenciling, and hand-paints furniture and walls.

Sponsor: North Shore Animal Hospital

Domini Canis

Artist: Sr. Janet Weyker, OP, Racine

Educated at St. Catherine's High School and Dominican College in Racine, Sr. Janet Weyker earned a master's degree in art education at the University of Wisconsin–Madison. She has studied calligraphy in Italy and England, has taught elementary and college art classes, and does freelance calligraphy and design.

Sponsor: Racine Dominicans

105

News Hound

Artist: Karen Johnston, Racine

Janesville native Karen Johnston received her bachelor's degree in art education from the University of Wisconsin–Madison and her masters of fine arts from Southern Illinois University–Carbondale, where she taught for two years. She also has taught art in K-12 settings, and was adjunct instructor at the University of Wisconsin–Parkside. Her ceramic sculptures have been exhibited in several Midwestern shows.

Sponsor: The Journal Times

Walt

Artist: Kate Remington, Racine

The proprietor of Remington-May workshop gallery, Kate Remington has been a practicing artist her entire adult years. Currently she spends most of her time working with concrete and cement. One of her favorite subjects is concrete animal portraits. In 2001 Remington completed 18 pet portraits, primarily dogs and mostly lifesize, in concrete and cement.

Sponsor: W. H. Pugh Marina

Labmap

Artist: Pam Christopherson, Racine

A lifelong Racine resident, Pam Christopherson is a graduate of Horlick High School and University of Wisconsin–Parkside. A stay-at-home mother active in her sons' school lives and in her church, her hobbies include cooking and baking, gardening and reading. She and her family enjoy Racine's many interests and activities, which led her to the design idea of Labmap.

Sponsor: Lighthouse Title Services, Ltd.

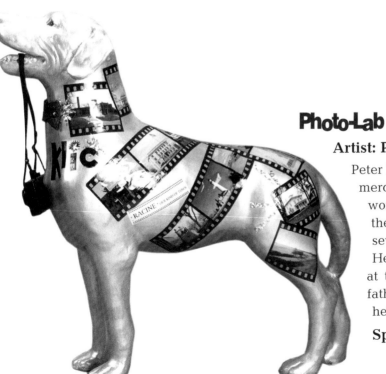

Photo-Lab

Artist: Peter Buchaklian, Racine

Peter Buchaklian is the owner of his own commercial photo studio, Clic Photography. He works with agencies and manufacturers in the Racine area. His background includes seven summers as director of a youth camp. He also teaches swimming and lifeguards at the Racine Family YMCA. Buchaklian's father, Sark, who works in his son's studio, helped with the creation of *Photo-Lab*.

Sponsor: Racine Family YMCA

Diversity Dog

Artist: Georgette Hardy Edwards, Racine

Georgette Hardy Edwards is a teacher in the Racine Unified School District. She is currently teaching at William Horlick High School. She attended University of Wisconsin–Whitewater, where she earned a bachelor of science degree and a master's degree in art education. Her primary medium is ceramics.

Sponsor: Greater Racine Coalition for Educational Excellence

Outandabout

Artists: Lorna Hennig, Jane Hitzelberger, Sue Ramagli, Michael Rude, Debbi Wiedenhaft

Lorna Hennig, a practicing artist, is executive director of the Racine Arts Council. Jane Hitzelberger designs spaces and makes unusual jewelry. Sue Ramagli, a photographer, is program director of the Racine Arts Council. Michael Rude, a massage therapist, is project director for the Racine Arts Council. Debbi Wiedenhaft, a bead artist, is a receptionist at the Racine County Convention and Visitors Bureau.

Sponsor: Racine Arts Council and Racine County Convention and Visitors Bureau

Barkitecture

Artists: Ann Curcio, Kelly Gould, Vicki Kalcic, Jill McCarrier and Jodi Soczka, Kenosha, Wisconsin

Barkitecture was the collaborative effort of five area artists. Kelly Gould, Vicki Kalcic and Jodi Soczka are alumnae of the University of Wisconsin–Parkside. Jill McCarrier completed her undergraduate work at the University of Wisconsin–Madison and obtained her master's degree from Cardinal Stritch University. Ann Curcio graduated from the University of Wisconsin–Oshkosh. *Barkitecture* was created using a variety of media and was based on Gould's concept drawing.

Sponsor: Korndoerfer Development

Priya (Beloved)

Artist: Irene R. Olson, Deerfield, Wisconsin

Originally from India, Irene Olson relocated to the US in the 1960s and practiced medicine in the Madison, Wisconsin, area until the 1980s, then moved exclusively to her other love—the world of art. Clay sculpture and watercolors are her focus. She owns The Blue Iris Gallery in Deerfield, Wisconsin. Her love of animals is reflected in her painting and sculptures.

Sponsor: Bombardier Recreational Products

House Pet

Artists: Coldwell Banker Agents and Staff, Racine

House Pet was conceptualized by Sue Causey and Linda Schubring, both long-time real estate brokers with Coldwell Banker Residential Brokerage. Assisting in bringing the vision to life were Katy Diekfuss, Reiman Publications, who did the landscaping art; Terri Sharp, Lori Destiche and Hannah Wosilait, all with Coldwell Banker.

Sponsor: Coldwell Banker Residential Brokerage

Home Is Where the Dog Is

Artist: Linda S. Godfrey, Elkhorn, Wisconsin

A freelance illustrator, author and cartoonist, Linda Godfrey holds an art education degree from the University of Wisconsin–Oshkosh, with additional studies at UW–Whitewater. Her works have been shown in numerous regional galleries and exhibits, and she has taught art in public schools in Sheboygan, Burlington and Lake Geneva. She currently works out of her home studio.

Sponsor: N. Christensen & Son

RACINE, The Alphabet Dog

Artist: Sybil Brauneis Klug, Lake Geneva, Wisconsin

Sybil Brauneis Klug works in acrylics and oils. Color is the primary focus of her landscapes, flowers and still-life arrangements. Her paintings have been included in juried shows at Wustum Museum of Fine Arts, Anderson Arts Center in Kenosha and Rotary Gardens in Janesville. She is a teacher at Fontana Elementary School. Her work can be seen at the GLAA Gallery in Lake Geneva, Wisconsin.

Sponsor: Bukacek Construction Inc.

111

Patriotic Pooches

Who says Labs can't be as patriotic as people? Not these four and the one shown in The Dogs Come from School.

"The…dog, in life the firmest friend. The first to welcome, foremost to defend."

—Lord Byron

Victoria

Artist: Jane Thronson, Franksville, Wisconsin

A former teacher of art and stagecraft in the Racine school system, Jane Thronson was also employed by a Chicago advertising agency in the production department and as an artist at University of Wisconsin–Madison designing promotional materials for the continuing education department. Most recently, she is crafting Americana pieces, lawn ornaments and nautical accessories in a variety of media.

Sponsor: Thermal Transfer Products

America's Guard Dog: Wrap Yourself in Freedom

Artist: John Kasprzak, Racine

Art has been a major part of life for St. Catherine's High School 2002 graduate John Kasprzak. He has done everything from creating simple pieces of art to animated shorts, and a monthly comic strip for the SCHS school newspaper. He plans to attend Illinois Institute of Art–Schaumburg to prepare for a career in graphic arts/animation.

Sponsor: Stephen and Judith Denning

Patriot

**Artists: Nancy Tyyska and
Jim Tyyska, Jr., Racine**

This mother-son duo works in a variety of media. Nancy Tyyska uses oil as her medium of choice while son Jim Tyyska works on the computer. Nancy is retired and enjoys travel and crafts. Jim is currently employed by Wisconsin artist Don Nedobeck. He has done art design and direction for various Web sites and also creates art for art's sake.

Sponsor: Nancy Tyyska

Sargey

Artist: Robert M. Bleeke II, Oak Creek, Wisconsin

A graduate of Carthage College, Kenosha, with a degree in graphic arts, Bleeke currently works as a senior page at the Racine Public Library. In his spare time he puts his artistic efforts into self-published comic books and children's book ideas.

Sponsor: Racine Public Library

Sports

Labradors love all kinds of sports. And so do the creators of these nine dogs, that represent everything from golf to race-car driving to motorcycles.

"Dogs are natural athletes. The sporting breeds... are after all jocks. They live to do what centuries of selective breeding have equipped them to do best: work out."

—Jon Winokur

Blaze

Artist: Bonita Carbajal, Racine

A native of Stevens Point, Wisconsin, Bonita Carbajal studied architecture and art history at the University of Wisconsin–Milwaukee. She works in oil, charcoal and watercolor, and does papier mache sculpture using recycled materials such as paper bags.

Sponsor: Joseph Swanson and Company

Hot Dog!

Artist: Christopher Sklba, Racine

A Racine native, Christopher Sklba is a graduate of Milwaukee Institute of Art and Design. A professional goldsmith, he has won several Midwest awards for his jewelry designs. Sklba also teaches adult education classes in metals at Wustum Museum of Fine Arts in Racine.

Sponsor: Seater Construction

Kelly

Artist: Heather Foster, Oak Creek, Wisconsin

Painter Heather Foster received her bachelor of fine arts degree from the Maryland Institute College of Art, Baltimore. Her work has been shown in exhibitions across the United States. Many of these paintings have been inspired by animals and their personalities. Kelly demonstrates the spirit of those dogs who dream of nothing but tennis balls with every cell of their bodies.

Sponsor: First Stepp Builders, Inc.

Hard-ly

Artist: Jeff Vlieger, Franksville, Wisconsin

Jeff Vlieger has been painting most of his life. He carried his artistic talent all the way through high school and in adulthood painted for enjoyment. Following an employment change he started painting motorcycles. He now does lettering and pinstriping for Hribar Corp. and continues to paint bikes and murals.

Sponsor: Jensen Metal Products

Dog-Leg Retriever

Artist: Jim Jedlicka, Racine

After graduating from the Ray Vogue School of Art in Chicago, Jim Jedlicka began his graphic design career in Chicago. After seven years, he accepted a position as a senior designer with a Racine firm. Since moving to Racine, he operated his own design firm, worked on numerous community projects and presently holds the title of design director.

Sponsor: Design Partners, Inc.

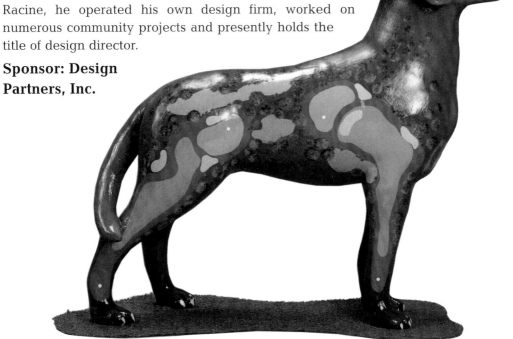

Lap Dog

Artist: Susan Silver, Racine

A graduate of the University of Wisconsin–Madison with a bachelor's degree in art education, Susan Silver is currently a member of the education staff at the Wustum Museum of Fine Arts in Racine. She previously taught art in the Wauwatosa public schools and also has done visual merchandising and displays for several retail businesses in Racine.

Sponsor: Charles and Joan Patton

Lake-Loving Lab

Artist: Penelope Grill, New York City and Racine

Penelope (Penny) Grill, a fine artist, graphic and Web designer, divides her time between New York and Wisconsin. A graduate of Washington Park High School, Racine, and Hollins University in Virginia, she also attended graduate school at American University in Washington, DC. Her works have been shown in a number of exhibits in New York.

Sponsor: Johnson Wax Professional

The Bird Dog

Artist: Renee Popadic, Racine

Born and raised in Racine, Renee Popadic has always enjoyed arts and crafts. As an adult, her favorite hobby is working with wood. She has focused her drawing, sculpting and painting talents to create wildlife woodcarvings. Popadic is a member of Racine's Wildlife Carving Club.

Sponsor: ERA Newport Realty

Diana

Artist: Louise (Sliv) Kasen, Racine

Louise Kasen, a native of Racine, attended Layton School of Art and has done oil and watercolor painting. She paints designs on doors, walls, ceilings, floors and furniture. Her signature "Sliv" appears on all her works.

Sponsor: Kasen, Patterson & Reback, S.C.

The Universe

The universe offers people answers to questions while raising many additional questions. The universe also offers the artist the opportunity to bring the universe down to earth, as these nine creations show.

"Then the sun god decided to create new people. First he made a man, then a woman, and finally a dog to keep them company."

—Folk Literature of the Tehuelche Indians

Sun Dog

Artist: Julie Lalor, Racine

The mother of three teen-age boys, Julie Lalor includes art, antiques, Racine history and gardening among her interests. She enjoys decorating and keeping her home in a constant state of change with her children's artwork and arrangements of her own design.

Sponsor: Ron Jones

El Dia del Perro Muerto

Artist: Alex S. Mandli, Jr., Racine

Born and raised in Racine, Alex Mandli is a potter whose works have been exhibited throughout the United States. His ceramic works have earned numerous awards at juried exhibitions. He has been an art instructor for many years and served as artist-in-residence for many schools in Southeastern Wisconsin and Northern Illinois.

Sponsor: Quick Cable Corporation

122

Canis Major

Artist: Pete Jedlicka, Racine

Pete Jedlicka is a graduate of St. Catherine's High School, Racine, and studied commercial design at Milwaukee Area Technical College. He has taken a ceramics class at Wustum Museum of Fine Arts. At home he works in watercolor, ink and marker drawings and in the future would like to work in furniture design and large abstract metal designs.

Sponsor: Racine Gymnastics Center and Peppermint Preschool Gymnastics

Celestial Dog

Artist: Stephen Samerjan, Shorewood, Wisconsin

Stephen Samerjan is an associate professor of painting and drawing at the University of Wisconsin–Milwaukee. His work has been exhibited nationally and appears in many private, corporate and public collections, including Wustum Museum of Fine Arts and the Long Beach Museum of Art in Long Beach, California.

Sponsor: Clifton Gunderson LLP

I'm Sirius!

Artists: Heather Bumstead and Marcie Molbek, Racine

Heather Bumstead and Marcie Molbek, both amateur artists, work for Lincoln Lutheran of Racine, Bumstead as a chaplain and Molbek as an activity director. Bumstead's favorite medium is "old-fashioned pencils on paper," while Molbek prefers "hands on" craft-oriented art, especially anything that will enhance the lives of Lincoln Lutheran residents.

Sponsor: Lincoln Lutheran of Racine

Sirius, Dog Star

Artist: Jo Anne Wood, Racine

A lifelong Racine resident, Jo Anne Wood has a degree in art education from the University of Wisconsin–Madison. A former middle school art teacher and children's book editor, Wood is now the co-owner and creative director for *Copycat*, a national magazine for K-3 teachers.

Sponsor: Lakeview Pharmacy

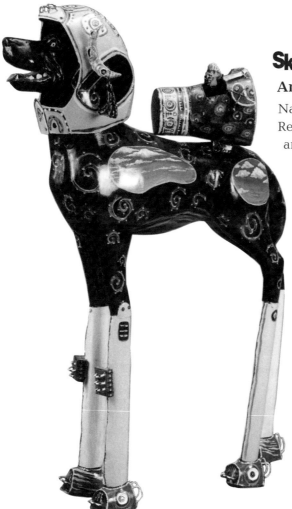

Sky Lab

Artist: Bill Reid, Racine

Nationally known sculptor Bill Reid received his bachelor of fine arts degree from Kansas City (Missouri) Art Institute and his master's degree in fine arts from Cranbook Academy of Art in Bloomfield Hills, Michigan. A graduate of The Prairie School, Racine, he also studied at Lawrence University in Appleton and in its program in London, England.

Sponsor: The Prairie School

Sun Dog

Artist: Robert W. Andersen, Racine

A Racine native, Robert Andersen has been an art teacher in the Racine Unified School District for 29 years and an active local artist for three decades. A graduate of Park High School, he received his bachelor of science degree in art from the University of Wisconsin–Whitewater and his masters degree in education from Carthage College.

Sponsor: Skipper Bud's Reefpoint Marina

Star Struck

Artist: Joan Houlehen, Cudahy, Wisconsin

A graphic artist/designer, Joan Houlehen is a partner in A. Houberbocken, Inc., an art consulting firm. Her works are in the Northwestern Mutual art collection and many other commercial and private collections. She is a docent at the Haggerty Museum of Art on the Marquette University campus and on the board of directors of the Friends of the Museum.

Sponsor: Eppstein Uhen Architects, Inc.

126

The World of Work

Everyone is somehow involved with the world of work at one point or another in our lives and experiences. As these 13 dogs and one in The Dogs Come from School show, the world of work can range from medicine to watches and other time pieces, to money and machinery, and more.

"They are playful companions…they are loving companions…they are health-giving companions…they are calming companions…and they still carry out their age-old duties of alerting us to intruders in our homes and protecting us from attack—to mention only two of their surviving work roles."

—Desmond Morris

Doggie Xpress

Artist: Chuck Torosian, Racine

Racine native Chuck Torosian was an art director and illustrator for leading advertising agencies in Chicago, New York and Los Angeles. Now semi-retired, he is active in the fine arts community. He teaches fine arts and marketing, creates advertising and develops artwork concepts for children's books.

Sponsor: Merchants Moving and Storage

Work Like a Dog

Artist: Julie Lynam, Racine

Julie Lynam attended the University of Wisconsin–Stout and earned a degree in art education. She now teaches art and is the student activities director at St. Catherine's High School. Her favorite medium is painting on canvas; however, she has donated her time painting furniture for the American Heart Association's Heart Ball auction.

Sponsor: Goebel Electric, Inc.

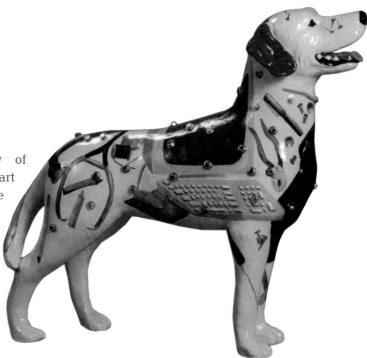

Chili—Begging for Bones

Artist: Cary Hunkel, Madison, Wisconsin

Cary Hunkel was educated at the University of Wisconsin–Madison where she earned her master of fine arts degree. She is a member of the Society of Animal Artists, and her watercolors and drawings have been shown throughout North America. She also has illustrated several wildlife books and articles. Her two active retrievers inspired her license plate—K9 KAOS.

Sponsor: Doug and Nancy Paulin

Acu-Dog

Artist: Arthur Shattuck, Racine

Dog Days of Summer is Arthur Shattuck's first venture into art for public healing. He has lived in Racine for more than 10 years, is a physician of Oriental medicine and a supporter of the arts. Shattuck continues to explore the relationship among healing, medicine and art.

Sponsor: Sheepish

129

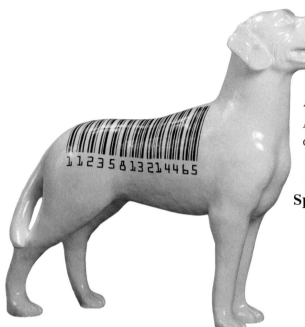

Barkode

Artist: Gary Wolfe, Racine

An interior designer who specializes in restaurant design, Gary Wolfe was born in Virginia and has lived in Wisconsin since 1986. He recently moved his design studio from Milwaukee to West Sixth Street in Racine.

Sponsor: Oh! Monah Design, Inc.

Good Watch Dog

Artist: Lenore Sydnor, Racine

Lenore Sydnor studied art at Syracuse University and the University of Wisconsin–Madison. She did graduate work at the University of Wisconsin–Milwaukee. She taught art for Racine Unified School District for seven years. Since 1974 she has owned and operated V.S.O. Ltd., where she designs and makes fine jewelry. Unusual and exotic gemstones are her passion.

Sponsor: V.S.O. Ltd.

Golden Labrador

Artist: Trudi Theisen, Monona, Wisconsin

Trudi Theisen received her bachelor of science degree from the University of Wisconsin–Madison. She has participated in numerous juried exhibitions throughout the United States and also held recent solo and dual exhibitions in Wisconsin. She is a member of several local, regional and national arts organizations and her work has received many awards.

Sponsor: M & I Bank

Good Buoy!

Artist: Barb Henley, Sobieski, Wisconsin

Barb Henley is a former art teacher currently working with alternative education students in middle and high school. She uses art frequently as a medium for self-expression with students experiencing difficulties in school and at home. She also coordinates mural design and application for Southeast Asian and Hispanic students during the summer months.

Sponsor: Jeff and Linda Waller

A Train-ed Dog

Artist: William G. Wald, Burlington, Wisconsin

William Wald and his family live in "Chocolate City." A self-employed custom cabinetmaker and designer for 15 years, Wald currently is enrolled as a full-time student at the University of Wisconsin–Parkside, where he is pursuing his bachelor's degree in art education.

Sponsor: Thermal Transfer Products

Hear Ye

Artist: Sr. Janet Weyker, OP, Racine

Educated at St. Catherine's High School and Dominican College in Racine, Sr. Janet Weyker earned a master's degree in art education at the University of Wisconsin–Madison. She has studied calligraphy in Italy and England, has taught elementary and college art classes, and does freelance calligraphy and design.

Sponsor: Quota International Club of Kenosha/Racine

K-9-3756

Artist: Trenton Baylor, Racine

Trenton Baylor's mechanically enhanced Labrador is an example of one of the many medical and technological advancements that in the near future will be able to save many injured dogs. Baylor is an assistant art professor (sculpture) at the University of Wisconsin–Parkside. He received his bachelor's degree from UW–Parkside and his master of fine arts from UW–Madison.

Sponsor: Karen and Bill Boyd

Watch Dog

Artist: Vicki Kalcic and Jockey Design Group

Artist Vicki Kalcic is the creative director at Jockey International, Inc. She considers herself fortunate to work with a talented group of graphic designers on various projects, including *Watch Dog*. Kalcic graduated from the University of Wisconsin–Parkside with a bachelor of arts degree in fine arts and had a studio at the Upstairs-Downstairs Gallery.

Sponsor: Jockey International, Inc.

Working to the Bone

Artist: Rachel Gedemer, Racine

Rachel Gedemer is a graduate of Case High School. She is currently a student at Columbia College in Chicago, pursuing a bachelor of fine arts degree, focusing on fashion design. Gedemer usually sketches and draws illustrations. Her work on the dog is her first experience with paints.

Sponsor: Earth Tech

The Wright Touch

Frank Lloyd Wright's influence is obvious in Racine's architectural landscape, as evidenced on these four dogs and the one featured in A Project in Process.

"Let Hercules himself do what he may. The cat will mew and the dog will have his day."
—William Shakespeare

Prairie Dog

Artist: Doug DeVinny, Racine

An art professor at the University of Wisconsin–Parkside, Doug DeVinny earned his bachelor of arts degree at Colorado State University and his masters of fine arts degree in printmaking from Indiana University. At UW–Parkside, he is also director of the Parkside National Small Print Exhibition. DeVinny's work has been displayed in many solo exhibitions and in several juried national exhibitions.

Sponsor: Porters of Racine

Prairie Dog

Artist: Tim Baumstark, Racine

Tim Baumstark holds a bachelor of fine arts degree from the Milwaukee Institute of Art and Design. He is the owner of Boxhead Design, a graphic design studio in Racine. Baumstark enjoys working three-dimensionally and vows to "resist the usual" in his creations.

Sponsor: Boxhead Design

Dog Gone Wright

Artist: J.S. Adams, Racine

A lifelong Racine resident and mixed-media artist, James Adams is known for his relief castings in paper, plaster and acrylics. He exhibits at regional art fairs and competitions, and has been juried into Watercolor Wisconsin at Racine's Wustum Museum of Fine Arts every year since 1996. He received his art education at Layton School of Art in Milwaukee.

Sponsor: SC Johnson

Frank Lab Wright

Artist: Meg Daniels, Racine

A part-time artist and full-time mom, Meg Daniels enjoys jewelry making, glass painting and furniture decoration. She trained in metal arts as an undergraduate at New Mexico State University and loves trying new art forms.

Sponsor: Willard and Mary Walker

137

Prize-Winning Dogs

While all the dogs on display in Downtown Racine's Dog Days of Summer are true winners, critters needed to be chosen for prizes of $3,000, $2,000 and $1,000.

Judging took place in early May. Frank Paluch, director of Perimeter Gallery, Inc. in Chicago, and Katie Gingrass, owner and director of Katie Gingrass Gallery in Milwaukee, spent several hours reviewing each of the 149 dogs. Using a point system, the pair rated each on the basis of artistic merit, craftsmanship and design uniqueness.

The three prize winners, who were notified prior to the release of this book, are:

First—*Trojan Dog*; artist Renee Staeck, Milwaukee; sponsor Landmark Title of Racine, Inc.

Second—*Dog Bone*; artist Linden Schulz, Racine; sponsor Inspec, Inc.

Third—*The Labrador of Lilliput*; artist Melanie Pope, Racine; sponsor Racine Public Library

Trojan Dog

Staeck, a Racine native and senior drawing major at the Milwaukee Institute of Art and Design, said in her dog design proposal that *Trojan Dog* parallels "the Trojan horse, used as a sneak attack during the Trojan War of 1260 B.C., according to *The Iliad*. With the *Trojan Dog*, cats are hidden in the dog decoy in order to attack their enemy—the dogs."

Staeck, profiled in the Other Critters section of this book, covered the dog's entire body with faux wood and mounted it on a wheeled platform. Several cats crawl out of the dog's back.

Dog Bone, found in the Leisure-Time Pursuits section of this book, "is designed for public interaction through its functionality as a chair," explained second-prize winner Schulz of Racine.

The owner of L.A.S. Sculpturewerks in Racine, Schulz said in his dog design proposal that "The dog will be cut in half and each side will be used to house the hidden steel structure while functioning as an armrest for the user. The bone-shaped seat and backrest members will offer users a place to rest their own bones."

While a senior at the University of Wisconsin–Whitewater, third-prize winner Pope of Racine created *The Labrador of Lilliput*, found in the Arts and Entertainment section of this book.

In her dog design proposal, Pope explained the dog's theme "is an adventure scene taking place in the town of Lilliput, where Gulliver had his travels. The dog belongs to Gulliver and like his owner is being taken over by the Lilliputians, but in this case by the children. They have turned him into a plaything."

Because of the extremely high quality of the creations for Dog Days of Summer, the judges chose to name 10 high honors and 20 honorable mentions.

High honors are:

Vinny, created by Kathryn Gagliardi, sponsored by Jim and Deanna Parrish.

Prairie Dog (In His Wright Mind), created by City of Racine Main Gallery Young Artists Program participants Katie Gebhardt, Jarrod Johnson and Cory Tuinstra; artist-in-residence Jane Hobbs-Cascio; sponsored by Jensen Metal Products.

Golden Days of Summer, created by Philip Krejcarek, sponsored by Mathis Gallery and Frame Shop.

Laughing Dog, created

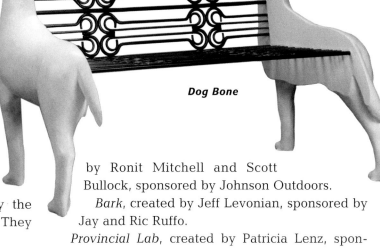

Dog Bone

The Labrador of Lilliput

by Ronit Mitchell and Scott Bullock, sponsored by Johnson Outdoors.

Bark, created by Jeff Levonian, sponsored by Jay and Ric Ruffo.

Provincial Lab, created by Patricia Lenz, sponsored by Twin Disc, Inc.

Sky Lab, created by Bill Reid, sponsored by The Prairie School.

Home Is Where the Dog Is, created by Linda Godfrey, sponsored by N. Christensen and Son.

Ain't Nothin' but a Hound Dog, created by Sandy Schmitz, Mary Ann Logic and friends; sponsored by The Cobblestone Ltd.

Bird Dog, created by Kate Smallish, sponsored by CRB Insurance.

Honorable mentions are:

Sam E. Dog, Adventurer, created by Ada James, sponsored by Gorman and Company, Inc.

Working to the Bone, created by Rachel Gedemer, sponsored by Earth Tech.

Gus—Goes to the Beach, created by Kevin Pearson, sponsored by Karen and Sara Johnson.

Chili Dawg, created by Pat King, sponsored by Robert W. Baird.

Snuggle, created by Krista Lea Meinert Edquist, sponsored by O & H Danish Bakery.

Reflections, created by Tanya Fuhrman, sponsored by SC Johnson.

Carmen the Star of CopaLABana, created by Pat Levine and Rebekah Levine, sponsored by Water's Edge Clothiers.

Bonne a la Bone, created by Bill Reid, sponsored by Samuel and Gene Johnson.

Puppy Tut, created by Kate Smallish, sponsored by Johnson Bank.

K-9-3756, created by Trenton Baylor, sponsored by Karen and Bill Boyd.

Barkitecture, created by Ann Curcio, Kelly Gould, Vicki Kalcic, Jill McCarrier and Jodi Soczka, sponsored by Korndoerfer Development.

Doggie Bag, created by John Kasprzak and St. Catherine's High School art students, sponsored by Quizno's Downtown.

Watch Dog, created by Vicki Kalcic and Jockey Design Group, sponsored by Jockey International, Inc.

Good Buoy!, created by Barb Henley, sponsored by Jeff and Linda Waller.

Toy Hound, created by Franklin Deracin, sponsored by Shear Madness.

Cock-A-Doodle Dog, created by Amy Zahalka, sponsored by Friends of Racine Heritage Museum.

El Dia del Perro Muerto, created by Alex Mandli, Jr., sponsored by Quick Cable Corporation.

Vincent Van Dog, created by Jay Harris, sponsored by Design Partners, Inc.

Hard-ly, created by Jeff Vlieger, sponsored by Jensen Metal Products.

News Hound, created by Karen Johnston, sponsored by *The Journal Times.*

About Downtown Racine Corporation

Mission Statement

The Downtown Racine Corporation will be the leader in the continued economic, aesthetic and recreational revitalization of Downtown and its neighborhoods.

We will be proactive in the retention of existing business. We will facilitate new developments by promoting public/private investments and partnerships, and working cooperatively with the other economic development organizations.

In all that we do, we will communicate effectively with our members, partners, many diversified neighbors and the public at large.

Vision Statement

Downtown Racine will be:

A symbol of the community's pride.

A center of celebration and recreation on the lake.

A harmonious mixture of residential, commercial, cultural, recreational and governmental activities.

A safe, convenient and aesthetically pleasing place to live, work, shop, visit and play.

Respectful of its historical character, its charm and waterfront setting.

Pedestrian and driver-friendly with efficient traffic circulation, signage and convenient and safe parking.

A unique retail center serving the needs of its neighborhood, the community and visitors.

People-oriented and neighborhood for all neighbors.

Downtown Racine Corporation Board of Directors

Chair
Brian Anderson
SC Johnson

Vice Chair
Lynne Ciaramita
Lakeview Pharmacy

Secretary
Julie Harring
Avenue Frame Shop

Treasurer
Kathy Bach
DeMark, Kolbe & Brodek, SC

Index of Artists

143

Index of Sponsors